THE MALE AGENDA

BARRY DURDANT-HOLLAMBY

First published in 2001 by The Art of Change
ISBN 0 9530063 2 8

A Cataloguing-in-Publication catalogue record for this book
is available from the British Library.

Typeset by:
David Brown, Maynards Green, Heathfield, Sussex TN21 0DG

Printed and bound by:
Windmill Press, Hadlow Down, East Sussex, TN22 4ET, England. +44 1825 830319

Printed on acid free paper from sustainable forests in Europe.

Published by:
The Art of Change
P.O. Box 441, EAST GRINSTEAD, RH18 5BH
www.artofchange.co.uk
E-mail: welcome@artofchange.co.uk

Other materials available from The Art of Change
are listed at the back of this book.

To all men everywhere

Acknowledgements

Do you thank everybody – or nobody? Do you risk forgetting some, while mentioning others? So many people have been a part of this book and of my own development that to name everybody would be a book in itself. As it is, a printed acknowledgement here can hardly come close to expressing my heart-felt appreciation to all those who have helped me along the way.

I have decided to take the risk by mentioning a few people. Many others have also been involved in my journey – to all those who have and who do not receive my public appreciation I thank you anyway. You'll know who you are.

My wife Winnie – my rock. Mother, lover, editor, artist and my very own therapist. Thanks for joining me on this adventure. Anna and Sophie – my daughters. For teaching me so much about how and how not to bring up children (I hope I'm getting some of it right!) and for reminding me of everything that is important in life but that adults often forget.

John and Margaret Durdant-Hollamby, for bringing me into the world, caring for me and teaching me the value of respect, honesty and friendship. Margaret again for your generosity in helping to make this book happen.

Kim and Noel Durdant-Hollamby for the fun we have

together as brothers and for showing me that, no matter how different we all are as people, your family can always accept you for who you are. Thanks to Kim also for the photography and design ideas.

Len Boon – my father-in-law, who has taught me that you are never too old to learn. And for supporting us unconditionally throughout the writing of this book.

Shelley Sishton – for your organisational skills, editorial feedback and inspiration. Ian Sishton for your support, designs and talent on the golf course!

The Forest Row 'men's group' – who taught me that men can laugh together, cry together, trust each other, love each other and release anger with each other without resorting to alcohol, drugs or workshops!

Steve Biddulph for the invaluable editorial advice and for the work he has already done for men, women and children worldwide.

Annique and Marco – for your friendship, trust and generosity – without your gift this book would not be in print.

Robert Holden for your inspirational work and your wholehearted support.

Jill Newton – for your valuable contributions as both an editor and literary guide.

Mark Lucas – for making me question the validity of this book and for sending me back to the drawing-board with it.

Ruth, Peter, Lara, Sheila, Claudine, Michael and Julia – for the wisdom you each share with me through our group.

The dads and young men from Forest Row who turn out, week upon week whatever the weather, to share each other's company around a football.

Costantino, Tim, Lesley, Caco, Peter, Angela, Simon, Nick and many others who have provided feedback and suggestions from initial manuscripts.

Alun for introducing me to my Mac. Keith Hagenbach for your proof-reading. Chris Price for your layout and artwork skills. Peter and David for your advice and work in printing this book.

And finally, all those people who have been brave enough to seek my help and in so doing have become my teachers.

Grateful acknowledgement is made for use of the following:-

The originators of quotes used at the beginning of chapters.

"The Calamine Lotion Path" contributed by Leon Nacson:-
http://www.theplanet.com.au
email: nacson@theplanet.com.au

"My Last Prostitute", "Fishing With Dad", "My Father's Hand"
and "The Death Of Mike" all stories contributed by the
"MensWeb" site:-
http://www.vix.com/menmag/menmag.html

Where stories appear, identifying details have been
changed where necessary in order to protect the identities
of those concerned.

Contents

Introduction

When I had completed an earlier draft of this book, I took some advice from an experienced author who suggested that I start showing it around to various people to get some feedback. As I handed out copies, I found that one of the main questions men had prior to reading it was, "Who is this aimed at?". I am sure that any reader would want the same question to be clearly answered; so, here is my answer.

First a little background. My primary role in life at present is as a husband and father. For the last few years I have also been working as an Intuitive Counsellor, helping individuals to discover and access their own inner strengths and truths. I live in a small corner of South East England where, with its high cost of living, I have experienced and observed many of the pressures that are placed on men's shoulders today. Pressures that probably exist the world over, regardless of location. The pressure of being a committed and successful employee; the pressure of being a caring and effective partner and father; the pressure of providing dependents with the means to satisfy an ever changing and ever more complex list of material requirements.

Whilst responding to these pressures, we find more and more that we are not fulfilling **our own** needs or desires – and this is being reflected by society as a whole. The world is not becoming a happier place. It is very possible that, in spite of our material comforts, we are amongst the unhappiest families ever to live on earth.

This book is aimed at those men who are struggling to 'hold it all together' and who are looking for some down to earth guidance and help. Those men who are badly in need of answers to questions that are a concern to all of us, men and women alike. Questions such as:

* Can a man today expect to be happy and have a family?
* Can a man today be a successful bread-winner and a good partner/father?
* Do men today **enjoy** being fathers and partners or would they really prefer to be out doing their stuff without the ties of a partner and children?
* What constitutes happiness and is it achievable?
* How much pressure does society place upon men to become something that they don't really want to be?
* Are men able to express what they feel? Do they even know what they feel and how important are feelings anyway?
* Do men really know what they want and do they, or can they, in fact do anything towards achieving those ends?
* Is there something we can all be doing to encourage the devel-

opment of a society that helps men to achieve a more balanced and enriched position within it?

A desire to find a few of these answers myself was the starting point for this book – a book that I hope will shed a little light on the path we take as men.

Many of the issues covered may also relate to women – but the spotlight here is on men. I have no intention of underestimating the difficulties and needs of women today, but my experience as a man makes me better qualified at this stage to examine the male point of view. I hope this book will be read by men and women alike, so that each can better understand the male position. A society which more fully appreciates what it is like to be a man today may end up providing more effective support to both sexes.

My challenge to any man who is feeling a degree of emptiness or dissatisfaction in life is to stop, look and take stock of the things that make you who you are. Your job, your family, the things that make you happy, the things that make you sad. The things that you would like to do with your life, things that you do not want to waste your time doing.

Just for once in life, try pausing. Think about what exists in your life today that has the potential to bring you happiness and satisfaction tomorrow.

The question of why have I written this book also merits an

answer. Through my work I have observed in many men a very high level of dissatisfaction with life. A dissatisfaction which is often not even recognised at a conscious level. Some men have described this to me as a feeling that somehow, somewhere, all is not well. Others have suggested a sensation akin to numbness. I would like to help men to recognise their numbness, so that they can bring feeling back into life.

I want to share with you my belief in the truth of the following statements:

* It's important to have dreams in life.
* It's fine not to have the answer to everything.
* It's not unusual to find 'feeling' embarrassing, difficult, and even impossible.
* It's normal to be scared of change.
* It's good to want change.
* It's alright not to be entirely sure who you are or what you are here to do, but it's also important to look for the answers.
* Working through your issues can be hard, heart-rending work but is ultimately, **always**, rewarding.

To help you to get the most from this book I would ask that if upon reading a particular section you find yourself 'feeling' something, be it joy, anger, sadness or excitement, think about what that feeling may be trying to tell you about your own life. Do not just jump onto the next section. Pause for a few minutes and consider what you have just read and why that may have brought up feelings in you. You may be surprised at what you learn.

A book can never contain all of the answers to the mysteries of life. But maybe, just maybe, it can give you the extra bit of strength you need to effect a change. And that could be the start of a chain reaction that ends up affecting many more people.

One word of caution before you start. If you are really happy with who you are, with what is happening in your life and the environment in which you find yourself every day, there is probably no point in reading this book, for you are unlikely to be seeking change. Neither is there much point in reading it if you're only doing so because your partner or friend has coerced you into it. As men we tend to resent, and therefore rule out, any information that comes to us under duress.

Read it because you want to; read it because you want to make improvements in your life; read it because you want to learn more about who you really might be.

1

What Does A Man Need?

"In the middle of the journey of my life I came to myself within a dark wood, where the straight way was lost."

Dante

What does a man need? The answers to this question are going to be different for every person. There are however some areas that most men will have in common. A happy and exuberant sex life would be rated highly by most men; financial security, another subject high up on the male agenda; a good, well-paid job is another aspect of life which is generally considered important.

Beyond these, however, a second level of needs exists. Needs that we don't talk about. Needs that are not generally understood or considered to be important by society. Needs that we may even be embarrassed by.

For example, the desire to hug and be hugged; the longing for companionship that is often felt by a man when his parents are no longer around or able to support him in difficult times; the need for someone to talk to about issues which may never be dreamt of in the confines of the pub or workplace, issues such as death or illness, family responsibilities, work pressures or affairs of the heart.

These and other needs have been ignored for so long that a man who may on the outside come over as a powerful, dominant and often unemotional human being, may retain on the inside all the elements of vulnerability and sensitivity that he had as a child.

Underneath the exterior of today's man, there may lie this sleeping self. A chameleon who has grown so used to his disguise, he no longer recognises himself. But a chameleon who would like to know his real identity and who, if he was really truthful, would love to show the other creatures around him what he really looks like.

JOHN AND SYLVIE

John and Sylvie, a married couple in their thirties, were at our house having dinner. Throughout the evening John would draw the conversation back to the boredom he was facing with life and in particular with work. "I'm going nowhere. I don't enjoy what I do and yet I have to do it to keep the lifestyle we have now; but then working that hard means spending a lot of time away from home and that means missing the kids growing up." A common complaint amongst our friends.

At this point my wife Winnie asked him what he would do if he won the lottery. (This is a great game for finding out who people really are!) He answered without a pause for thought: "I'd become an archaeologist and travel the world". Sylvie, his wife of thirteen years who thought she knew everything about her husband, gaped at him in surprise. The chameleon had shown his true colours.

Tribal Instincts

We have come a long way since the days when the men would gather together to go off hunting for their tribe, leaving the women and children at home, to return days later with their food and tales of the successful and unsuccessful parts of their trip. In such times, whole villages would share in the fortunes and misfortunes of each individual and family. An illness suffered by one was supported by tens, maybe hundreds. A successful story was heard by the whole village or tribe and recognised accordingly. A problem was shared, not just by the partner, but by a community. Man and woman, through their individual talents and skills, be it in hunting or medicine, in teaching or mothering, were able to respect and value the strengths and weaknesses of each other.

How does that compare to our society today?

Today, a man may still go off for days or weeks at a time. He will generally be the only representative from his 'tribe'. Instead of bringing home food at the end of his trip, he will generally be rewarded at a later date with money. He will come back to either his own lonely accommodation, or to a house where his wife and children, although pleased to see him return, will neither thrill to the tales of his adventure nor share immediately in the physical rewards of his conquests. In fact, the rapturous and victorious welcome that was prepared for his ancestor is replaced very often by a begrudging reception that almost seems to imply resentment of the fact that he has been away at all.

Today, the extended family and tribal support network, so important to male and female alike, has disintegrated. Because of this we have lost much of the support that men and women have enjoyed in the past. Families tend now to meet up occasionally, rather than daily, and very often under such time constraints that a meaningful sharing rarely takes place.

This fragmentation of our society may be more damaging than we realise. I believe that men are desperate to be acknowledged and understood and yet many of us don't understand ourselves. On the one hand we are seeking recognition for what we do or achieve, and on the other hand we are seeking to recognise who we are.

We want our problems to be understood both at home and in the work-place – and yet both places may offer quite conflicting solutions. We want to have our desires accepted. We may, at a much deeper level than we are consciously aware, want to share our emotions with a broader section of the community than just our partner or therapist. But when we look for those supporters – if indeed we do – what we tend to find is a society of independent units containing a number of isolated individuals each fighting for his own survival.

Men have suffered greatly as a result of this isolation. At a deep level we have become virtually friendless, often dependent upon our partner for our only emotional support. And even then we find ourselves unable, untrained, to make best use of that support. So many of us have been brought up to demonstrate to everybody else that we're fine and we can cope, when the truth may be very different.

How do we communicate that truth? We don't. Men have become great editors of information, broadcasting what we think people want to hear whilst cutting out anything which may seem unnecessary – such as feelings. We spend so much time on 'transmit', showing the world we're fine and the life and soul of the party, that we may have forgotten how to 'receive' – either from ourselves or someone else.

As a result, we could be blanking out all sorts of information from which we would benefit (other people's feelings, problem situations forming) choosing instead to present a surface image of perfection. And when we are not busy presenting ourselves to others, we speed back to a life of 'doing' which continues to prevent us from 'receiving'. And then we find ourselves expressing shock when the problem we have been failing to observe finally surfaces.

There is much to be done to repair the damage; fortunately there may be much that can be done. There is nothing to stop entrenched patterns being changed. Neither age nor health need be a barrier. We need to repair the holes in our families; we need to take the initiative as men to show that the family, all aspects of it, is of immeasurable value to us. For it is through those closest to us that we get the best chance to see and find ourselves.

Do you find time to share with your parents, siblings and children (by sharing I mean open and honest two way communication)? Do you have the patience to listen to them? Could you help them to help you become a man who transmits and receives openly and without fear?

COMING HOME

Gerald was in his eighties and had just suffered the loss of his wife of 40 years. A hole suddenly developed in his life: no-one to shop for, no-one to walk with, no-one with whom to share holidays or concerts. Although he lived within a few miles of various members of his family, he did not want to burden them with his sadness and loneliness. He remained in his house, unconsciously denying his need for companionship and support. His health soon started to deteriorate as he gradually lost the desire to live.

Gerald's daughter became aware of this worsening decline. It became clear that Gerald had a major health problem and he soon found himself unable to cope. Although he had initially resisted the idea, Gerald soon found himself being housed and cared for by his daughter and son-in-law.

Over the course of the next two and a half years, Gerald went through various medical treatments, all under the watchful eye of his family. As his health improved, his progress was witnessed by his grandchildren who began to benefit greatly from his wonderful stories and experience of life. He started to 'transmit' his feelings more and more and was able to 'receive' in a way that helped him to open his heart to his family. In an environment that encouraged this sharing, he found himself immensely valued and deeply trusted.

Gerald gradually became a 'fixture' in the house, and is now enjoying excellent health, driving himself around and regularly taking part in family outings and holidays. He has let go of his other house, and has given up many of his old belongings in order to be able to stay with his 'new' family. His downward spiral has been halted and he has demonstrated that we are never too old to change.

Checklist:-

1) You have just won the lottery. You have all the money you will ever need. After meeting any material needs that you may have, think about what you would do with your life. What would you do to satisfy yourself, and how does that relate to what you are doing today?

2) If you go away on business, look out for an opportunity to bring back something that you can share, from the heart, with those closest to you. This may just be a story, or a description of a place. Value what a lift your own experience, when shared, can give to those around you.

3) Make the time to meet with family members and be prepared to be on 'receive' rather than on 'transmit' all the time. See what messages you pick up about their lives that you have maybe been missing.

2

What Goes On Inside
A Man?

"There is another man within me, that's angry with me,
rebukes, commands, and dastards me."

Sir Thomas Browne

We start off our life sweet and innocent. We start off trusting everyone and everything, knowing that all our needs will be met. Ideally, we have been carried around in a safe and warm place for nine months and in our early months most of us experience the love and affection of our family. We have no reason to mistrust the world around us. In nearly every baby can be seen perfection – the embodiment of love.

At this early point we have hardly been conditioned at all by outside influences. However, as we begin to grow and develop, we begin to absorb the attitudes, emotions, anxieties, joys and anger of those nearest to us. Parents and family inform us, through their own actions and responses, that there is a general lack of the things they crave the most.

Time, money, love. As we move into our teenage years and into early manhood, we have come to expect that there will not be enough of these commodities, and so are not surprised to find the lack of them entering our life. We have been programmed by the influences and attitudes of the world in which we find ourselves.

It is entirely possible that part of our 'life experience' involves absorbing information and then seeking confirmation that this information is valid. After all, assuming life is an evolutionary process and we are in some way meant to grow or develop, it seems clear that our desire to grow must be fuelled by something. The desire to find 'our truth' may well be that something. It is entirely possible that the man you are today is partly due to the attitudes, behavioural patterns and third party experiences that you have absorbed in your life up to now. How your father treated your mother, for instance; how society has taught you to treat illness; how your parents have taught you to think of money or love.

All of these ideas may be important pieces of information that we carry with us through life and we use to help create our identity. As we absorb this information, I believe we will then seek out verification that this information is correct. That is to say at some level, whether consciously or not, we will go and seek a corresponding experience that supports the information we have been given.

So, let us say for example that over the years you have been told by your parents and family and friends that your life is destined to be one of poverty and ill health. That no matter how hard you work, you will always struggle to make ends meet. The likelihood is that you will go out and find proof that this is true, not necessarily because you want to at a conscious level, but because this is what your conditioning is instructing you to do at a much deeper level.

All the time that you do not question the validity of this instruction, you will be guided towards finding this 'reality'. And find it you will. You will find that life is full of poverty and that ill-health also seems a necessary part of existence. Those men who have achieved riches from a poor background, or health from a background of illness, may well have done so as a result of challenging those very beliefs.

We have become conditioned in many different ways, some of them beneficial, many of them not beneficial. Our internal 'programme' does not judge anything to be right or wrong, in the same way as you can enter any type of information into a computer and it will not judge some information to be unacceptable or bad. Our programme merely accepts this information and then seeks out opportunities to validate it. Such validation will generally depend upon an answer; confirmation, in the physical world as this is the realm that we can relate to 'objectively'. Hence we find we are attracting all sorts of unwanted physical experiences due to information which may be many years old.

Can We Change This Information?

Yes. We have free will. What do I mean by free will? We have the choice to allow or not allow anything into our lives. Right now, there is nothing that can stop you from changing anything about your life that brings stress or discomfort. You may think there are plenty of reasons and I am not for a minute suggesting that you immediately quit your job, leave your partner or take up rollerblading. I am just saying that there is nothing that stops you from doing any of these things. You have free will. You can change whatever you want.

The same goes for our internal conditioning. We can 'reprogramme' ourselves. If we don't like things that are regularly entering our lives, then the best place to start is by beginning to change the messages that we are putting out. To have success with this process it may not even be necessary to delve into the past for traumatic events or deep-rooted attitude problems that go back to childhood influences. It may be no more complicated to start with than sitting down with a pen and paper and writing down the things that we would like to start experiencing in our life now.

Personal Sabotage

A man in black breaks into your office late one night and re-programmes your computer so that it malfunctions in a subtle, but very destructive way. Several weeks later, after much despair, you discover the change in the programme. How do you decide to fix it? By trying to work out how you could travel back in time and try to stop him from changing the pro-gramme? Or by putting the correct programme in now?

How do we change that programme or conditioning? In my work with men it has become clear that identifying what it is that we want in life is often a common stumbling block. It is extraordinary how so few of us may really seem to know what we are living for. And yet how can we expect to be happier with our lives if we don't even know what would make us happy?

One way of finding out what it is in life that we do want may be through the identification of those things in life that we fear happening to us. It is interesting how often finding out what you don't want will lead you to a clearer understanding of what you do.

By writing down our fears we bring them into consciousness and make it that much easier to seek the opposite – something that we would really like or enjoy. Let us suppose, for instance, that you fear running out of money. It's a very common fear. Now let us turn that around and identify exactly what it is that you want money for. "I want the money to…" (list those things precisely that you want money for now). Envisage each item clearly. As you do this you will find that the thought of having the money for that specific purpose (or purposes) gives you a powerful and positive feeling. It is from such a base, a positive one as defined by love as opposed to a negative one as defined by fear, that you start to create your new conditioning (a more detailed breakdown of this exercise is given in the 'Tool Kit' section at the back of this book).

Through this straightforward process, fear is acknowledged and then becomes the tool which leads us to where we want to go. Fear becomes our friend, our guide. There is a saying that "fear is only ever love disguised".

Do not be put off by an intellect that tells you that you have no fears. Many men think they fear nothing, only to find out subsequently that they have many fears they are not addressing. We all have fears. Fear of death, fear of redundancy, fear of not being able to pay the mortgage, fear of never having children – all common examples. Once you start being honest with yourself you will find there is plenty of information from which you can start to make changes.

MICHAEL AND SARA

Michael and his partner had been trying to have a baby for many years. They had been through all the tests, tried orthodox and unorthodox means, but had still not managed to conceive, and no-one could locate a problem.

Social pressure had combined with their own lack of clarity to produce a very tense situation. Michael felt the backlash of many barbed comments from colleagues questioning his sexual ability. To a man an inability to help conceive a child is often judged as the ultimate sign of failure. In the end they made contact with me to see if there was a block in their thinking.

In our first meeting I suggested we look at what fears existed in their lives. At first Michael in particular found this challenging, and was unable to list anything about which he was fearful. Sara, his partner, was not so shy in coming forward.

"I fear never having a child. I fear having a child and losing the life that Michael and I have together. I fear the danger in the world that this child is being brought into. I fear that if I don't work we will not have enough money to do the things we want to do. I fear becoming a 'housewife' and having to go to coffee mornings. I fear not being able to travel so much. I fear giving birth. I fear ante-natal classes". The list went on.

Michael remained relatively silent, although he was clearly quite astonished at the depth of Sara's feelings. I encouraged Sara to start making these fears into things that she really wanted. "I fear giving birth" became "I want to trust my body". "I fear the danger in the world" became "I want to feel safe". "I fear losing the life Michael and I have together" became "I want to enjoy my life to its maximum potential". "I fear not being able to have a child" became "I want to be able to have a child at the perfect time". And so on with the others.

I then asked them to think about how this list would look if they put it in order of priority. Their greatest want first. There was a silence. A long silence. Neither of them felt clear that the greatest priority at that time was in fact having a baby. There was clear uncertainty between becoming parents and enjoying their lives and freedom as they had been used to.

I suggested that, until they were absolutely clear that their greatest desire was having a child, conception might itself remain uncertain. Being a very caring couple, if they had conceived and subsequently had a child, they would almost certainly have experienced great confusion and guilt at times when they found themselves putting their own needs ahead of their child's.

This recognition of their truth, through the listing of their fears, was like a huge weight lifting for Michael and Sara. I was basically helping them to give themselves permission to stop thinking that they had to have a baby. They both realised that it was okay not to be certain that they wanted to start a family yet. They have since let go of their fear of not having children and are currently still assessing their needs and desires. In the meantime, they're really enjoying life.

Checklist:-

1) Be prepared to challenge any limiting beliefs that you have acquired throughout your life.

2) Consider change in any area of your life. Don't necessarily make any changes immediately, just think about them. Remember when you limit change to certain things, you may be stopping the good stuff from getting even better! Be open to all possibilities.

3) You are in charge of your life, no-one else is. Start taking responsibility for everything.

4) Use your fears to guide you into a clearer picture of what you want from life.

3

The Power Of Thought

"And I have felt

A presence that disturbs me with the joy

Of elevated thoughts; a sense sublime

Of something far more deeply interfused,

Whose dwelling is the light of setting suns,

And the round ocean and the living air,

And the blue sky, and in the mind of man."

William Wordsworth

Quantum physics suggests that all matter is in essence vibrating energy. Whether it is a brick or a pane of glass, a man or a mouse, a fly or a lump of concrete. All of it is energy vibrating at different rates. The denser the material, the slower the vibration.

More recently, scientists have also demonstrated that the thoughts of the observer in a quantum experiment will affect the outcome of that experiment. Matter responds to the observer's thoughts. This would appear to indicate that thought is a powerful energy, an energy that vibrates at a higher speed than matter. We may well be in the preliminary stages of acquiring scientific proof that thoughts can control matter.

The implications of this very simple explanation when applied to our lives could be far reaching. Think about it. Thought affects matter. Could it therefore follow that what we think can affect how our bodies react? Could it also follow that what we think could affect things that happen to us, even what environment we find ourselves in?

There is now a new field of medicine which is called 'Psychoneuroimmunology'. In simple terms this is the science of mind over matter – a process in which our thoughts have some sort of control over what happens to our physical bodies and particularly the immune system. Many books have been written on the subject and some of the leading specialists in illnesses such as cancer are great advocates of mental techniques such as visualisation, meditation and positive thinking. They are beginning to make use of the discovery that improved immune responses are clearly linked to a positive and relaxed approach on the part of the patient.

Very often these advocates are medically trained specialists. People who have learnt from their experiences that there is not a material cure for everything. Recognised scientists who are looking to the power of the individual's mind to play a major part in the healing process.

Men will quite often find such suggestions challenging. Why? Because this is not something that is easily measured. We like results, and we like to know where these results have come from so that we can duplicate positive results again and again.

We also don't like to risk making fools of ourselves on something that is so intangible. We have become so cut off from our feelings and intuition, that it has become very difficult to trust ourselves to improve our physical wellbeing by virtue of a change in attitude. Most of us have been brought up to ignore our intuition; to do what we think we should do instead of what we want. Is it therefore any surprise that – having failed to listen to our feelings thus far in life – we find it difficult to accept that those same feelings may now have a major role to play in our lives?

And yet we will all have had many experiences in life that have already demonstrated clearly the strength of our most powerful thoughts. Often men have these types of experiences when we are young, and as we get older we lose the belief that we have much control over our happiness or health.

As we get older we are conditioned to believe that dreams cannot come true. We learn that it is misguided to believe that you can have what you want, and so we stop thinking about what gives us a good feeling and take instead what we think we must. Everything has a cost it seems. Ideals take a battering. Dreams often get squashed by harsh parenting, desire gets blunted and life becomes a sequence of events and experiences which are sometimes bearable, sometimes not, punctuated by the occasional completely joyous moment.

My experiences and those of many other people working in the field of the mind/body connection have shown us the importance of our individual desires and joy. Whether it is in the relief of suffering for someone dying or in the acquisition of a material object by someone who previously believed it to be unobtainable, we are witnessing how an understanding of the mind's part in creating our own reality is imperative in achieving our goals. It is my belief that we, as men, are quite willing to accept this role of the mind but that, quite understandably, we want proof first that there is good reason to believe in it.

This proof we can find now in many different forms. We will have experienced many occasions in our lives ourselves when the mind has enabled us to achieve something that we wanted.

STEVE

Steve had been through a very difficult time in his life and wanted to reduce his financial liabilities. He had decided either to sell his house or rent it, and move to a less expensive area. His quandary was which to do. Sell or rent?

I asked him to focus on this particular question. I explained how powerful thoughts are and asked him to be clear in his own mind exactly what it was he wanted to know. I suggested that if he did this he would not necessarily need to 'do' anything to acquire the information he needed – the information might just become clear.

The next morning at 8.30 my phone rang. It was Steve. He told me that half an hour previously an old friend had called him 'out of the blue' and had explained to him how he had been renting his house to three tenants who had just vanished owing several thousand pounds in rent. Within the space of 24 hours, and without 'doing' anything, Steve had received the information that he had been seeking – from a completely unexpected quarter – that would help him decide to sell.

Further evidence of the role that the mind can play can come through accounts of other people's experiences and books. There is so much information available today to show the scientific value of the correct use of thought that we are doing ourselves an injustice if we do not at least consider the evidence that is available.

HARRY

Harry is a professional man in his late fifties and had recently been diagnosed with cancer in two organs. He and his wife had had meetings with two leading consultants and had come away from these meetings feeling pressurised into taking some sort of immediate action; unfortunately the consultants were suggesting different courses of action.

I introduced Harry to the concept of quantum physics and gave him various evidence to study. Books, articles, case studies – all information which helped him to see the potential of the mind in healing. It was suggested to him that he learn first how to focus on what he wanted to achieve, which at that particular time was a clarity of mind regarding the conflicting advice being recommended by the two consultants.

He learnt to meditate, read more and started being aware of what messages he was giving out to people. To start with he had been desperate (understandably) to do the 'right' thing (that is, take the right medical route) – and people were responding to him in an equally desperate way (as shown by the sense of panic and disagreement from the consultants).

Now he was learning the importance of taking the action that 'felt' right at a time that 'felt' right. He focused his attention on choosing the consultant who made him 'feel' good. He attended his next meeting with this consultant in a more focused state of mind. The consultant, possibly responding to Harry's decrease in fear, did not push him into anything. This alone was a significant change from previous meetings. It gave Harry precious time to reflect, read more about his illness and find out more about potential benefits and side effects of the treatment being recommended.

Upon careful consideration of all the information available, Harry and his wife were able to make the choice of treatment that seemed most appropriate by all concerned. A need to satisfy an initial intellectual panic had been replaced by a desire to act in a more careful and considered way.

This story has no magical fairy-tale ending. However, Harry has found that since he has started to understand a little more about his own potential he has been able to attract far more of what he wants into his life and far less of what he doesn't want. For many cancer patients life becomes something they can no longer control. For Harry, it became one of the first times in his life that he had taken control of what was happening to him.

This he has achieved by being clear in what he wants. It is inevitable that every cancer patient wants their cancer to go and Harry is no different. But he is also aware that he cannot possibly judge what he still has to learn from this experience.

Instead of being in a maelstrom of panic he tries to assess everything clearly and in relation to how he feels. Since becoming aware of the potential of his own thought processes, Harry has been able to take life-changing decisions without the effort and anxiety that he would previously have assumed to be necessary.

What was the big change for Harry? Accepting that he had some involvement in his condition. Accepting that there was some point in getting really 'involved' in his own progress. That to remain as a spectator whilst the doctors got on with his repair work was never going to create a satisfactory solution.

Accepting that we have some involvement in our condition can pose a big problem for men intellectually – after all if we are unhappy or ill or stressed it indicates some sort of failing on our part; that somehow we are to blame for our unhappiness or illness. But this is only a very small part of the picture.

If you take it to its logical conclusion, what this evidence really suggests is that we have the power to change those things that are happening to us that we do not wish to have happening to us. In other words, by understanding the importance of the mind and our thoughts in our present state of being, we can take back control of our lives. As soon as we realise this, we are stepping out of the victim mentality and into a life where we may very soon start to see both the physical and mental repercussions of an improved and more positive approach to living.

If we do start to realise the power of the mind, which is a hard battle for some men because we are such concrete thinkers, we will want to find ways to use our thoughts in a productive and positive way. We will want to see results. We will want to know that we are not on some crazy spiritual journey that is going to lead us to chaos and the derision of others. This 'knowing' can only come through personal experiences; experiences that will happen more regularly the more we connect with our feelings. We need to treat this approach as our own personal scientific investigation – using our male thinking skills to evaluate each experience as it arises. In this way we may gain a far greater understanding of what makes us tick.

Learning to let go of your need for measurable results and of your attachment to specific outcomes, will enable you to remain more open to this approach (covered in more detail in Chapter 10). Do not under-estimate how difficult it is to learn to let go.

Our most powerful thoughts connect very much with our feelings. They will bring to the surface emotions ranging from fear to happiness, from sadness to anger. Think of an experience you would like to have happen and you will witness a very positive feeling. This is what creating is all about for creating what we want in life necessarily revolves around thinking about what we want to have happen. Without knowing what it is we do want, we cannot expect to achieve a happy and satisfying existence.

Inner Guidance (Intuition)

I believe that we each have an inner guidance, a truth that represents what we are really here to do and achieve. Our ability to hear this inner 'voice' is one of life's challenges. It is my experience, and that of hundreds of thousands of others the world over, that this voice is most easily heard through periods of time spent in silence. It is heard more easily by allowing yourself to become more of a 'human being' and less of a 'human doing'. If you never stand still for long enough, it is less likely that you will ever hear what it is your body's 'intelligence' is trying to tell you (this 'intelligence' is part of the same intelligence that fights off infection, clots blood or regrows a broken nail).

When this failure to hear a message happens continually, when we regularly miss the messages that are passed to us every day through our emotions, it is possible that the body tries to give us a physical sign. This may well be through the vehicle of illness. It can start as a small irritation but if it continues unheard then it may soon grow into something much more obvious and sometimes dangerous.

PAUL

Paul was a successful businessman with a young family who found himself working longer and longer hours during his early thirties. He suffered regularly from colds, flu and occasional pains in his chest.

He rested for as little time as seemed absolutely necessary when he had an infection or cold, and would often go back to work at times when he was still clearly far from better.

Paul continued to ignore the signals that his body seemed to be giving him. His stress levels increased as did his feeling that somewhere inside something was not quite right. Not having been taught to trust his feelings however, he ploughed on regardless. Ploughed on that is until the day he keeled over in agony and was rushed as an emergency into hospital where he was diagnosed with a collapsed lung and made to take several weeks' rest.

Regular daily periods of silence (meditation) enable us to function more effectively at both a physical and mental level. They allow the mind to settle and enable messages to be passed through the body and, if necessary, into consciousness. These messages will not be like a voice, but may result in a clear feeling to act in a certain way.

You may experience more 'coincidences' in life, events that seem to guide you towards a particular action. It is worth considering that you may not be having any more 'coincidences' than you have ever had; it is just that your increased sense of awareness, brought on by regular periods of silence, is enabling you to observe these events more clearly. When this starts to happen, it is the proof that you have started to pay attention to your guidance, a guidance that is in every human being regardless of race, creed or social standing.

And did anyone ever tell you about this guidance? Probably not, not because anyone was keeping anything from you, but because they didn't know at an intellectual level that it existed. It is only now, with mass consciousness beginning to change that these ideas can even be discussed. Indications that mass consciousness is changing can be found everywhere; 'new-age' topics are common dinner party conversation; national newspapers and magazines are devoting larger spaces daily to alternative life styles and practices; even businesses are finding that their long-term future lies in meeting the public demand for environmentally-friendly products and organic produce.

This guidance is nothing strange. I am not talking about any weird, spiritual phenomena, just the plain old clues that are fed to us every day about our lives through the one vehicle we can trust above anything else – our emotions.

We may have been underestimating the value of our emotions. They will often have an answer for us that the intellect has been unable to provide. They are in fact the only thing in life of which we can be absolutely certain. When we feel happy, we are happy. When we feel sad, we are sad. Everything outside of our feelings is information and information is not something you can feel. We need someone else to validate that information as being correct. Not so with feelings – no-one else can tell us what we are feeling or why. Our feelings, our emotions are unique to us. One problem many men are faced with is not knowing how to access these feelings.

Still Waters

Imagine a lake. Imagine that your life is that lake, and that at the bottom of this lake there sits a treasure chest containing the answers to your life questions. Your mission is to locate the chest and find the treasures within.

Most of us live hectic, frenzied lives. You are probably the same. This has the effect of stirring up the water in your lake, making it impossible to see anything. It is only when you start to have regular periods of silence that your water can begin to settle down. And as it becomes still, so it becomes easier to see into. You will start to have greater clarity.

The more you practise, the easier it becomes to still the busy water and the easier it becomes to spot your treasure. It is inevitable that as you practise this more and more, so you will gain greater and greater clarity. Gifts of intuition will come to you and you will soon start to make far better use of your own hidden treasures. Without the periods of silence, without time to reflect and be still, your waters will remain muddy and agitated.

You can call this meditation, reflective listening, soul time – whatever you like. The name is irrelevant. What is important is that it will give you the opportunity to learn from the greatest teacher you will ever have: you. A brief introduction to meditation is given in the 'Tool Kit' section at the end of the book.

DEN

When Den first came to see me he was suffering from anxiety and panic and had been diagnosed schizophrenic by a doctor and psychiatrist. He was in his early twenties and it appeared

he had been sliding downhill over the preceding years. He was on very powerful drugs for his condition, a situation which he was told was likely to continue throughout his life.

Den was introduced to meditation immediately and encouraged to read some of the scientific evidence which indicates the physical benefits of meditating. He was impressed, although because of the drugs he was on he found it very difficult to take in much of this information.

As he continued to meditate, so Den began to find that his mind was becoming a little clearer as to what he wanted and what things upset him. This clarity he found very encouraging. Before he had learnt to meditate his thoughts had always been just a jumble.

Being a typical young man impatient to run before he could walk, he would lapse now and again from his periods of silence, picking up his recreational drugs and old bad habits. The truth began to dawn on him, however, that when he stopped working on himself, when he ceased meditating and stopped thinking about things that would make him feel good, he found he sunk very easily back into his old depressed, anxious ways.

This experience told him that he could change things negatively or positively by his own choices. He was excited to discover that as he focused on the things that made him feel good, and as he continued to meditate, so he found that the things he didn't want in his life began to decrease.

One example of this was his council accommodation which he hated. I asked him to focus on having a nicer house to live in, with pleasant neighbours (he was being harassed by some very aggressive neighbours at the time). Intellectually he found this idea to be rather absurd, but because he was doing so well in other areas he decided to give it a go. Three weeks later, 'out of the blue', Den's council contacted him to offer him his own small cottage in a rural setting, but close enough to a town for his needs. He really could now trust that he was playing a part in what was happening to him.

His need for constant support lessened as he found new strength and desire to live within himself. A few weeks later Den reported feeling happier more often than feeling depressed.

Within a few months he was taken off his medication entirely (by his doctor and psychiatrist who advised him to keep up with his meditating) and immediately felt the benefits of a clearer, drug-free mind. Should he remain free of treatment the NHS will have been saved many thousands of pounds. In addition the State may no longer need to support him for the rest of his life due to the decline that had previously seemed inevitable.

Checklist:-

1) Don't underestimate the power of your thoughts – particularly those that have a strong emotion attached to them. Use them to help create an improved life.

2) Be aware of the type of messages you are giving out to people. Try to act in a way which 'feels' right. A good way of doing this is to drop the words **should** and **ought** and replace them with more positive words like **want** and **choose** (e.g. instead of doing something because you **should**, try to find a reason why you might **want** to do it. If you can't find any reason why you would **want** to, you need to question your motives for acting against this inner guidance).

3) Don't be a victim of life any more. Be a creator and start with your thoughts.

4) Look out for regular signs of ill health which can indicate that you may be missing some sort of inner message about your life.

5) Read up on meditation, or talk to friends and colleagues who practise it. You may be surprised what you find.

6) Try sitting in silence (meditating) at least once a day (preferably twice) for fifteen minutes, allowing your thoughts the chance to become calmer and clearer.

4

What Does Success Mean To You?

"To laugh often and much; to win respect of intelligent people and the affection of children; to earn the appreciation of honest critics and endure the betrayal of false friends; to appreciate beauty; to find the best in others; to leave the world a bit better, whether by a healthy child, a garden patch or a redeemed social condition; to know even one life has breathed easier because you have lived. This is to have succeeded."

Ralph Waldo Emerson

As men we have a particular ability for focus in our actions and for being direct in our reasoning – no better necessarily than women, just different. These abilities can be very useful at times, but on other occasions can cause us to forget the initial reason for doing something (e.g. you may have first taken a job because you were motivated by a particular aspect of the work rather than for purely monetary rewards. Several promotions later you may find yourself working in a sector that doesn't inspire you so much in order to maintain a higher standard of living that has come with each promotion).

If we are unhappy we find we can use these abilities to our advantage, focusing on a hobby or our career and thus sheltering ourselves from having to face our distress. We often call this 'getting on with it' and it can sometimes be very useful and constructive for putting some distance between ourselves and an upsetting event. The downside of this is that, as a result of becoming immersed in something else, we may pretend that everything is fine, when in reality it is not. And it probably never can be if we are searching outside ourselves for any long term solutions to our individual happiness.

Success may be one area where we look for outside satisfaction. But what, in reality, is success? Who measures this and who decides what makes a successful man?

Time after time we hear about men who have become very 'successful', only to burn out at a very early age, drop dead suddenly, leave their families, walk out on work or become alcoholic. And yet, in society's eyes they often remain 'successful' due to their past achievements. Is this a real mark of success? Is this a standard that society recognises as acceptable? Is this what we want to achieve ourselves?

The pressure placed on a man to do exactly this is great. We live in a society where success is measured in mainly material terms and any failure to achieve a certain material level is considered a lack of success. It is clear that society exerts enormous pressure on each of us to conform to its criteria for success. It is not easy to stand up and say that you won't be pulled along in the same way as everyone else.

JIM'S STORY

Four years ago Jim and his wife Eva gave up their high-flying City life in favour of trying to make a living as cattle farmers. They went to the country, taking their four young children with them. Here's Jim's story.

"Swapping a generous city salary for a farmer's wages has been challenging. We're getting by, thanks mainly to a very understanding bank manager, although I can't yet pay myself regularly. Still, money seems to be quite low now on our list of priorities.

I have had to reassess my values and so has the family. For instance the time I used to take over my appearance when I was working in London is now spent doing things around the farm and with the family. New clothes? I can't remember the last time I bought something new. The executive saloon car has been replaced by a more practical vehicle, a van. The children have had to exchange their private education for the local primary school.

In many ways it's been bloody hard. Anyone thinking of changing their lives as radically as we did please take note. But there is no doubting in any of our minds that the pros far outweigh the cons. For many reasons, I believe that I am happier than ever.

The long days that I used to work in the City seem a lifetime away now. And it's not that I didn't enjoy much of it – I loved the first ten years or so and I seemed to have boundless energy then to do the work. Being out entertaining until three a.m. and then back in the office by 7.30 am was not unusual.

Of course the downside was that I hardly ever saw my children. At weekends I was so exhausted that all I wanted to do was rest and sleep. And so I missed out on quite a bit of my two eldest children's childhood. But I didn't think I could do anything about it – the pressures on me were so great to keep going.

During my thirties I started to change. My enthusiasm for the work started to wilt and all around me I witnessed colleagues who were suffering from the pressures and burdens of work in the City. At home, Eva was struggling more and more with the responsibility of bringing up the children. After much discussion, we decided to move to the country, from where I would commute to work.

The rest of the family was much happier living in the country. For me it was dreadful. I became an even more part-time father, spending much of my day travelling. Five years was all I could take. After many lengthy and intense talks we decided to throw caution to the wind and take up farming.

Our family had some experience in farming and we spent a long time looking for the right place. We ended up bidding for a run-down farm at an auction. Our bid was successful. Then the real work started.

The culture shock was enormous. With great trepidation, we bought a few cattle and started our business. We converted a shed into a small farm shop and Eva began growing organic vegetables. It's hard to describe the amount of work that was involved, but it was a burden that became almost too much when I injured my back and Eva had to do much of the manual work. She went from having immaculately-manicured finger-nails to having biceps like a navvy.

It was a crash course in farming for us and we have made

plenty of mistakes. Financially it's been horrendous, but things have been getting better. That is they were, until the foot and mouth crisis hit the farming community. Who knows where that will yet lead us.

I have worried about the effects of this dramatic life change on all of us. But if Eva's reaction is typical then I suppose I need not worry so much – she says that a million pounds wouldn't get her back to the City.

The effect on the children has been equally astonishing. They were normal, middle-class kids who thought that money grows on trees, but now we can say to them, "You can't have that because we haven't any money", and they understand immediately. In spite of occasional lacks, they have a wonderful life. They run freely all over the farm and their favourite toys include such wonders as an ancient toy tractor tied to a bicycle.

They are frequently covered in mud. In many ways it seems like the perfect childhood. They have their father back – I'm often here when they come back from school. They have made many friends, and there is more freedom for them than London because they can be more independent here. Everyone looks out for everyone else's child.

Me? Well, the repercussions of the foot and mouth crisis continue to be horrendous. Consequently my life is far from worry-free at this time and like all farmers I will be continuing to assess what changes we may need to make to continue. But on another level, whatever happens now I know that I have experienced life in a way which has brought me far more meaningful satisfaction and joy than anything I have previously done. Whatever happens in the future, no-one can take that experience away from me."

In the story above, Jim regards himself as "happier than ever". He's had the big income and the important job, but now he says he's found happiness. Could we, the males in society, regard this happiness as a measure of Jim's success? Can we really view happiness as a key ingredient in measuring success?

The likelihood is we would judge his lack of material wealth and possessions as proof that he was not successful. The likelihood is we would judge that his so-called 'happiness' was brought on by a dismal and reluctant acceptance that this is what he was now stuck with and so he may as well try to be happy – after all what else has he got. "Well, no, I'm sure it's nice for him," and similar comments would abound. "That's O.K. for him, but I'm living in the real world."

Well, what is this real world, and do we really want to live in it under its present structure?

War Time

Imagine this. It is war time. Your country has been overrun by the enemy who are setting up prisoner of war camps, in the shape of businesses. Certain lessons have been learnt from previous wars and the enemy has developed a clever strategy for converting its opponents into its allies. It makes promises of future rewards and happiness. It allows families to stay together for certain periods of time, as long as the man offers devotion primarily to the workplace.

Sometimes the enemy even fools the man into believing that he is working for the common good and that provided he goes on devoting his time and energy to his work, he will be able to reap his rewards fully in his later life. To keep the man an ally, the enemy offers teasers and small rewards in the shape of wage increases, an extra day off, a Christmas bonus, a promotion.

Before long, the man has been sucked into the enemy camp. The family, at first resistant to the lack of his presence, soon become accustomed to his presents. They begin to crave the improved lifestyle, bigger house, better holidays, faster car, and tell him how much more they now want. He knows the only way to get more is to work harder. He goes deeper into the enemy camp.

All the time this is happening, he is becoming more detached from his truth. His family, once so understanding and giving, becomes a constant source of despair. At the same time as it may be unconsciously projecting greater financial requirements and therefore pushing him out to work even harder, the family may also be requiring more attention and emotional support. He looks to the other people in the 'enemy camp' for guidance. He sees people working even harder, carrying their burdens and trying not to complain. This is the way it must be, he presumes.

The enemy, being clever, provides him not only with rewards but also with a therapist. The therapist takes him through his life, allows him to see how his mother is to blame and his father, and their parents, and his school teacher – and sends him out each time thinking that at least he is not responsible for this unfortunate feeling of inadequacy. Knowing that it is someone else's fault relieves him of some of his burden for a while – although therapy meetings tend to become more regular and less effective.

All this makes him feel less like he can do anything about his situation. His observations tell him that everyone is in the same boat. He begins to notice how his co-workers tend to come into work on a Monday morning relieved at leaving their families behind. He gets dragged further and further into the illusion that he cannot be a man and expect to meet his own needs or those of his family under any circumstances. And so he gives up trying. He stops listening at all to his own internal signals, he switches off from the damage he is now inevitably inflicting on himself and his relationships, and he becomes a complete member of the enemy camp while still believing that the enemy are bastards and that he *has no choice. The only problem is, he no longer knows who the enemy really is.*

It may not be so far fetched as it may sound on first reading. We now find ourselves in a society where we, as men, are encouraged to become independent as soon as possible so that we may start 'fulfilling our potential'. We gather our degrees or apprenticeships, we become informed in one subject or another, and go blindly into the world thinking that a decision that we may have made as early as 17 years old, was absolutely correct. All too often, we force ourselves to carry on an occupation and lifestyle that is in no way connected to our true feelings of the moment.

The Good News Is...

...there is no enemy. The only 'enemy' we will ever come across is the enemy that lies inside ourselves when we fail to acknowledge what it is in life that **we** truly want.

True, we have established an economic system that solely wants us to earn and spend; but we must remember that **we** have established that, and **we** have the power to change that. Those changes can happen at a societal level only if some of us start to introduce change at a personal level first.

When we do start to listen to our feelings, when we do find

those things that really make us feel good – be it building a tree-house for the kids or spending a night dancing instead of working – then we are starting to live again.

It is a man's instinct, passed down through generations, to gain the trophies and prey that society consider of value. Our male ancestors would come back from their outings with the very things that they and their dependents needed at the time. This may have been food, or wood or animal skins for clothing. They were guided by their needs of the moment and not derailed by thoughts of what they might need at some distant point in the future. Their success was measured in the moment.

Today, success and recognition is usually measured in financial terms. Of course there are plenty of people who are successful who do not have large sums of money, but for most men in our consumer-orientated society, acquiring material wealth is a guaranteed way of being viewed as successful, of achieving recognition. Money has therefore become a completely acceptable and worthy prey to hunt. For many of us it is almost the only worthy prey today.

It is no surprise then that we have found ourselves going out, on a daily basis, hunting something that we can never entirely capture, that could escape from us at any time in the future without warning, and which by itself offers no form of sustenance or physical gratification.

Sometimes it is necessary to find out 'what is' by finding out 'what is not'. Maybe that is why we have created many of these diversions: to find out what the truth really is. Our view of success and money and all their trappings is one such diversion. Our new life can begin with a simple truth; that success is a worthy prey only if we know to what end we want to be successful and how that will benefit ourselves and others.

Man's success today is often seen in the size of his mortgage, the number of cars, the private schools in which he can educate his children, the clothes he can buy, the type of golf club he belongs to. The material list is endless. Wouldn't it be good if his success was viewed in terms of his own feelings of happiness and fulfilment in addition to these material gains?

There is nothing wrong with wealth and power. Great things can be achieved with them, great enjoyment can be had as a result of having them. But I question whether they can benefit us fully if we have sacrificed our happiness and peace of mind to get them. We need to look for the balance between material wealth and mental and physical well-being – they do not need to be mutually exclusive.

We strive for success, but why? What are we going to do with it if we ever feel we've got it? Ask yourself that question before you set off on the next rung of your career ladder. What are you doing? Something you really want to, or something that you feel you have to or should? Why are you doing it? Because it brings you great satisfaction at both a mental and physical/material level, or purely because it pays the bills? Who are you doing it all for? You or everybody else? And if you really want to help everybody else, is it not possible that you might do this best by becoming clearer yourself in what your definition of success really is?

A PERSONAL STORY

I used to work in the music business. For 11 years I worked my way relentlessly up the ladder chasing 'success'. From tea boy to sound engineer to record producer. No clear reason why I wanted this success. Just seemed like the thing to do.

When Winnie gave birth to our first child, Anna, via emergency caesarean, I found myself experiencing a whole range of emotions I had never previously felt. The sadness of going off and leaving these two vulnerable people that I loved. The loneliness I felt climbing into the car in the morning, knowing that Winnie, who was still physically weak from the operation, was going to be coping with a baby whose timetable for rest and feeding was unlikely to fit in neatly with her mother's.

At that stage I didn't want to look at it all too hard. I kept on working for something that would eventually prove elusive. And all the time, I couldn't help feeling that I was somehow missing out on something that was happening right under my nose at home. The development of a family.

The music business contracted during the recession and, after much discussion and self-examination, I decided to give it up. Feeling more aware of my desire to be closer to home I took up one thing I felt I could do without qualifications. I started weeding gardens – a job that, though not intellectually challenging, enabled me to work hours that were far more harmonious with family life.

Our second child, Sophie, was born soon after. Her birth was extremely traumatic for both mother and child and again made me realise the value of life.

I closed my business down for three months to help look after them, and Anna, following the birth. Debts mounted. Banks were understanding, but interest and mortgage payments soon piled up.

I went back to work with new determination. Before long, I had turned my little garden maintenance company into a successful landscaping company getting more and more lucrative contracts. And yet as the contracts got bigger, so did the bills. I found myself working harder, under more pressure, and yet bringing no more money home at the end of the day than when I had been doing basic weeding with little pressure.

Then something happened to change everything. A throat condition, that had been building up for a year or so, encouraged me to look at everything I was doing in a more holistic way. I began to realise that I was chasing something that didn't even exist – validation from out there that I was someone. Validation from out there that I merited attention. Validation from out there that I was a good person. The only way I felt people would really approve of me was if I became successful.

I started to question everything in my life. I loved my wife and children, that I knew. And I knew that I had been leaving Winnie with far too much of the job that I wanted a part of. Raising a family.

I closed down the landscaping company. I spent a lot more time with the family. I started helping people with health issues and found I had a talent for inspiring others to deal with their fears and stresses in life. The throat condition improved dramatically and in addition it seemed that the more I followed my happiness and I stopped thinking about having to earn money, the more money came into my life. Not masses. But enough to have life as we wanted it.

In the years since then I have completely changed my understanding of what I used to view as success. I have received incredible support and countless words of thanks from the many people I have helped. In fact I received more encouragement from others in my first few weeks of my 'new life' than I had in the whole of the previous fifteen years. A few of the more personal successes of recent years would include:-

1) Being able to take and pick up both my daughters on their first days at school and on most days since.

2) Being there when Sophie's first tooth fell out.

3) Being able to say "yes" to a close friend who had suddenly found himself without anyone to help him move house.

4) Being there regularly to help with supper and sit down and share the day's events with the whole family.

5) Being able to play golf, tennis, music, football on numerous occasions, with the full support of my family, when I would previously have been 'chasing success'!

Spending Money

Like success, money can play a very important part in our lives. It is something to be used and enjoyed. It is a very powerful subject to discuss and inevitably brings up various issues for men.

This section is about the spending of money. Spending money can give us a feeling of power and authority. Even when we may have very little, taking our partner out and buying a present or meal can give us a feeling of being in control. Sometimes we'll do it even though we know we may get ourselves into debt that could be difficult to repay (e.g. "I'll worry about that when I get the credit card bill"). Ironically, the extra pressure these debts create can ultimately end up doing even more damage to our relationships.

Time and time again many of us repeat the same pattern of spending when it would be better not to, or spending to make up for something that we have failed to do or that we have done wrong. And then we are often surprised to find that instead of getting fixed by our cash injection, life has disintegrated a little bit more.

Like success, money has become a tool that we can use to assert our authority in the world. A device which says that we are somebody. The way in which we consume and spend our money has become a statement of who we are: "Look at me, I have this much money, I am of value". It is an outer expression of something that we are craving inside – to be of value to people that we care about.

Money has become one way in which we relieve ourselves of the work involved in achieving self-approval. If other people thank us for our financial support then surely that will be proof enough that we are approved of and therefore a good person.

THE CHILD WHO HAS EVERYTHING

I always thought I grew up in a "perfect" family. We had a huge house and garden, fabulous holidays abroad, and paid help to maintain the house/garden/cars. My mother didn't go out to work. My brother, two sisters and I attended the best private schools. My father worked hard at his office job. I knew he did it for us, his family, but it took him away from us a lot. He must have spent at least fifty percent of his working life travelling away from home. When he came back each time he brought plenty of presents for us all. Sometimes I felt guilty about all the stuff I was given. Christmas and birthdays brought a virtual embarrassment of riches. Dad just loved buying us things. I now understand that it was his way of showing his love for us – perhaps to make up for the fact that he could not hug us or ever say "I love you".

Now I'm 50 and I realise my dad has never really known who any of us are at all. I've been surprised at the strength of the anger hidden away inside myself all these years, and have only recently begun to release it and move towards forgiveness. Most of all I feel sadness – for my father, my family and me for all that we missed out on.

It is very common to find men whose only way of expressing their value to their family is by buying extravagant presents, holidays, houses, or bailing out members of the family who have got into financial problems. Because the family grows up accustomed to this behaviour it becomes a habit that neither party is able, or willing, to change.

Although the expenditure may make such men feel good for a little while, the feeling is likely to be short-lived and they will soon look for the next opportunity to buy someone something. The purchase produces a short-term feeling of approval, but once more this feeling fails to last and again the same sequence of events will ensue. And yet ask the family or partner what they would really like from the man in question and you might get an answer such as "a decent conversation with him" or "to know what he's feeling" or "to have a hug sometimes".

Money has become a tool upon which many of us have become dependent for occasionally producing in us feelings of self-worth and value. Unfortunately these feelings are likely to be short-lived, for we can never feel completely happy with ourselves when we only seek approval from others. The one way to feel really contented with life is to find that contentment within. To approve of – and be happy with – yourself.

Many men say that if they just had the money, happiness

would follow. Money can be a wonderful thing and I do not doubt that money can help us to create great happiness. But it is not necessarily true. History is littered with stories of wealthy people who were not happy. Money needs to become our tool, something which we use creatively. We must not be tempted to ascribe our unhappiness to the lack of money in our lives. I believe we have to find happiness now, with life around us exactly as it is, money or no money.

Checklist:-

1) What do you view as success? Material gain is fine, as long as it is in harmony with your values. Have you been aspiring too much to material gains at the cost of your happiness?

2) Where are you getting your fun from? Are you getting enough at this time in your life?

3) Money's great, but only if you know what you want it for. Don't just work for money, consider in detail what your financial needs/desires are. The thought of those things will help to create a good feeling and this is a much better place from which to go to work.

4) Don't be tempted into using money as a way in which to relieve yourself of the work involved in developing self approval.

5) See money as your tool, not your master.

5

Selling Our Present For An Illusory Future

"...trust no Future, howe'er pleasant!"

Henry Wadsworth Longfellow

How much is man encouraged today to spend his valuable energy thinking about and saving for future needs which may never arise? How much do we as a society allow each other to live in the present and enjoy all that it entails? How much do we as a society encourage hard work and long hours now so that we may have enough to fall back upon in the future? How much do we encourage the pursuit of happiness now as opposed to it being something that we might attain at some future point?

Many of us work on the understanding that we are 'building

up a future'. And yet all around us there are men who demonstrate how frail that understanding may be.

COLIN

Colin is a professional man in his fifties who had worked tirelessly all his life in order to provide his family with the funds necessary for private education, upkeep of a beautiful house and income which will enable him and his wife to start enjoying themselves in his retirement.

At least that was the plan. A couple of years ago, almost in sight of the winning post, Colin was diagnosed with cancer. All his planning crumbled around him as he absorbed the truth that he had spent his life in a career that he had stumbled into rather than chosen, in order to earn a reward he may never totally receive.

One of the reasons primitive man may have paid so much attention to the present, and so little to the future, may have been that he understood at some level he could not possibly anticipate what his future needs would be. As such he worked to achieve what was necessary, rather than what might prove to be necessary. It is only recently in terms of world history that so many of us have been in a position to accumulate countless material possessions.

'Stuff' which, so often, ends up being a burden and a liability.

Of course there is a balance to strike between the needs of the moment and our future requirements. We must, for instance, in the interests of future generations continue to invest in the safeguarding of our planet when making important global decisions. I am not suggesting that we act only with present moment needs in mind. We could self-destruct very quickly. But I am suggesting that at an individual level many men focus too much of their energy worrying about the future and therefore sometimes miss an opportunity in the present.

How many of us today could honestly say that we are not increasingly governed by fears of future deprivation and hardship?

Many of us put off doing something that would make us happy today because we may need the money tomorrow. We often delay saying something positive to someone today on the basis that there may be a better time. Many of us even suffer financial hardships and bills in the present whilst contributing much needed finances to a financial scheme that may provide us with some income in thirty years time if we are still alive.

The truth is, we have no knowledge as to what may be our needs at any time in the future. We work hard all our lives, putting our own real happiness on hold until retirement, based on the knowledge that then we will be able to relax and enjoy the fruits of our labour. And what happens? Some of us never even make retirement age; others are too incapacitated physically to be able to enjoy retirement; others find the family has long since split up into fragmented, unhappy units; others have put off fun for so long that real enjoyment becomes a mystery.

What does this tell us about putting off happiness and enjoyment until some future date? It tells us that this perception may be misguided.

If we could encourage each other to change our individual and collective view of success and money, we might halt the disintegration of a society that is so in need of change. If we could again realise the value of the extended family and community support network, the value of everyone from our elders to our children, we could once more achieve personal and collective growth and understanding through sharing. If we could redress the balance between our needs in the moment and our needs in the future, maybe we would find ourselves creating a 'now' that contained many more satisfactory and rewarding experiences. A 'now' that could lead to an even better future than the one we are so busy planning.

As an individual you can start this change from future projection to present moment awareness by asking this question:

"In what way am I every day meeting my own desires and needs?" If enough individuals start asking the question, society itself stands a chance of positive change.

Checklist:-

1) Start to think about all those things that you've been putting off but that you'd really like to do (whether it's telling your dad you forgive him, climbing Everest or clearing the attic!).

2) If it feels comfortable, try taking small steps towards doing one or two of these things. Whether it's making a phone call or taking a holiday, if the thought of it makes you feel good, don't underestimate what good may come from the event itself.

3) Look at how you can redress the balance in your life between living in the future and living in the present moment. Start to address your needs of today as much as your anticipated needs of tomorrow.

6

The Need For Balanced Information

"Where is the life we have lost in living?
Where is the wisdom we have lost in knowledge?
Where is the knowledge we have lost in information?"

T. S. Eliot

ROBERT

"Hey have you heard about...". How many times does a 'man to man' encounter start with these words almost invariably followed by some item of national or international doom and gloom news?

I gave up watching the news a number of years back but found that just to survive in my business I had to keep a smattering of knowledge so that I wasn't totally floored by this intro-ductory question when meeting clients. What kind of guy fails to watch the news, keep in touch with world affairs, have their finger on the pulse? The inference being that someone who doesn't must be inferior.

My attitude is a stark contrast to the home environment I came from. The constant background buzz of the media there as company to my lonely parents, and my father's obsession with the news.

Each morning he would wake to Radio 4 on his alarm clock, then move from his bedroom to the kitchen where the radio and mini TV would be switched on. Then to the living room to the main TV for breakfast news, to the car where, you guessed it, Radio 4 once again meets and greets, then to work at his dental surgery with the radio on all day while he drilled and filled his patients' teeth, and then home either to watch TV or go to some political event. Always tuned to the outside, always the news channel. He didn't take the paper except on weekends – he never had the time!

I would like you to ask yourself some more questions. When was the last time you sat through a whole edition of the news and came away feeling really good or more empowered to take positive action? When was the last time that you picked up the news-paper and thought how pleasing those front page stories were? When was the last time you went off to work in the morning having digested the morning news and thought how lucky you were to be living in this wonderful, caring and safe world?

The news industry has grown through the generations and the development of vast international news companies. In times of war news items became of great importance to keep a nation up to date with its progress. And yet even then the importance of national or international news was often put into perspective at a more personal level. For instance, reports which carried news of victories in battle could do little to lift the spirits of a family who had just received a bereavement notice. Their news, their 'real world', suddenly became very different to the so-called real world of the news broadcasts.

Like Robert in the story given above, I used to watch the news every day. I used to take newspapers and read daily what a terri-ble place the world is, what dreadful people there are all around us. It is only in the last couple of years, since I have substantially reduced my intake of news, that I have realised what a negative and numbing effect this part of the media had been having on me.

What is it about us men in particular that makes the news so important? What is it that makes us feel that the news has some vital bearing on our everyday lives? What is it that makes us feel that we are being irresponsible if we do not watch or read the news? Are we afraid that we will somehow lose touch with the 'real' world?

The questions I would like us to consider are these. What is the real world? And how much of the news that we watch, listen to or read has any relevance to what is happening in our real world?

Men have a great intellectual appetite for what is going on 'out in the real world'. We have made billionaires out of the bringers of news. We become fully engaged in disasters that are befalling others. We absorb large amounts of information relating to crises that may be happening in parts of the world we have never even heard of, let alone visited.

Consequently we may offer a certain amount of help, by sending a donation or loving energy such as saying a prayer. Often, however, we seem to get much more involved at an intellectual level. We put forward to our family and friends our own solutions to the problems. Problems over which we have no control, in which we play no daily part, and which may only serve to draw us away from the real problems that are affecting us directly in our daily lives. The news may have become another barrier that we use to hide ourselves from our own truths.

The argument that we are being irresponsible if we do not

study the news in detail does not, I believe, carry any weight. You would need hundreds of televisions all firing different news items at you twenty four hours a day if you were really to keep up with all the news that is happening in the world. We do not help those who are suffering by wasting valuable energy reading about them or watching them continuously. Unless we are one of those people who devotes his life to helping directly the world's needy, then the way that we can best help those who are suffering may be by helping ourselves, our families and our own community first.

We may have many different reasons for keeping up with world events, but we must remember we are being shown a tiny percentage of what is happening and of that percentage probably a fraction of 1% has any relation at all to us. What's more, because bad news sells, we are generally absorbing mainly negative information. Put this information into its purest form according to quantum physics theory and you have energy. Since this is generally bad news we are discussing, you could take this further and say that bad news is possibly representative of negative energy. Do you ever come away feeling good from reading these stories? It could be that you are absorbing negative energy every day without even realising it. This is something you could start changing immediately.

Every day millions of us absorb this negative information. We do not even question it. Our desire to be responsible, informed human beings may have coloured our perception of what is important in our daily lives. It seems that as many of us are addicted to this daily absorption of negativity as others are to drugs. We have become accustomed to the feeling that the news helps to give us our own place in society.

I believe that continual updating from the news makes men feel informed and important. The need to feel informed is one thing – the need to feel important is quite a different issue.

At work our importance is there for all to see. But at home, we are just dad, husband, lover. It is possible that this constant connection to important world events gives us a feeling of power again. Discussing wars, stock exchange crashes, deaths, seems to lend weight to our discussions and may help to make us feel more important. But is this because we feel that without these important events to discuss, we would have nothing of significance to say to our partners or family? Is it that we do not consider discussing such things as our feelings or thoughts, interesting enough for anyone else to hear? Is it that we feel empty without the stimulus fed to us through papers and broadcasts, so empty that we feel we have nothing of value to contribute?

The news can also be used as a barrier. A barrier that prevents proper sharing from taking place. Ask some men about their fathers and you will often hear tales of men stuck behind broadsheets, or of faces glued to news bulletins on the television. The news is commonly used as a way of avoiding meaningful contact with the people we most care about under the pretext that domestic problems are unimportant in the bigger world picture.

Better Use Of The News?

Imagine how you might feel if, for the rest of the week, you reduced your input of news and introduced more positive action such as reading a good book, taking a few walks or sitting down with the whole family to a meal. It may seem like a scary thought to start with. But it's also possible that you will find yourself enjoying life more.

You may find yourself going off to work in a quite different frame of mind each morning. You may find yourself talking to your partner and children more and enjoying it, instead of cramming in conversations between coming home, dinner or watching television. You may find yourself taking part in a far more rewarding sharing with those people that are closest to you. You may find yourself working through problems instead of avoiding them. You may find yourself feeling generally happier and less stressed.

And yet by doing this, by absorbing less information, you will not suddenly have become an uncaring man. You will not suddenly have become an idiot with no understanding of world problems. You will not suddenly have become a social outcast. Neither will you find that your performance at work is adversely affected.

You may find that changing your relationship to the news in this way may help you to make better use of the news that you do take in, finding ways in which you may really want and be able to help. You might even find it in you to effect one small change in your own life that leads to much greater happiness for someone close to you. Paradoxically, this one alteration in daily life could help you to become an even **more** responsible human being.

By seeking to understand fully where our responsibilities begin and end we can fulfil our own purposes that much better. As we spend a little less time worrying about what is going on 5,000 miles away with people we've never known and are never likely to meet, we may become more aware of what is going on very close to us. Consequently we gain greater awareness of the various problems and joys that our life is bringing us. Turning our back on our own personal problems, replacing them with far more 'important' issues such as world news, will never make them go away. It just postpones the time until they will inevitably have to be faced.

It is worth remembering that our own problems and those of

our family are the most important problems that exist in our 'real world'. This is where we have to focus our attention if we are to serve mankind in the best way that we can. We cannot expect to see peace and happiness in the world if we cannot provide it fully for ourselves under our own roof. Our own life is our battlefield and it is up to us to find peace here if we want there to be any reflection of peace around us 'out there'.

News is important. It has a vital role to play in society. It is the spread of information. If we can use this information effectively, by turning our reactions to bad news into positive action where desirable and detaching where not, then we will all benefit. But, like success, money or the future, we must not let news control us. We need to remind ourselves that fulfilling our potential is not so heavily dependent upon studying the world news as it is dependent upon our own clarity of mind.

Two questions to end on.

1) Do you have enough stimulus in your daily life to replace some of your news input (if not, what does that tell you about your life)?

2) Do you think you could achieve greater clarity in your life if you did reduce, even by a small amount, your intake of news. If you

are in any doubt as to the answer to this question, then surely it's worth trying a change anyway!

Checklist:-

1) Consider limiting the amount of negative information you absorb everyday. Try cutting down for a few days on newspapers and news broadcasts.

2) In the time you now have free, introduce something into your life that makes you feel good – perhaps a walk, sport or gardening.

3) Listen more closely to the 'news' that those closest to you bring every day – the stories of their lives. Be prepared to share your 'news' too. Look to your immediate environment as the 'real world' that most needs your attention right now.

7

Helping Lust To
Become Love

"Ho, pretty page, with the dimpled chin

That never has known the barber's shear,

All your wish is woman to win,

This is the way that boys begin.

Wait til you come to Forty year."

William Makepeace Thackeray

The Influence Of Pornography

I am heterosexual and this book is therefore written from a heterosexual standpoint. I would like to think, however, that many of the issues covered, including some of the points raised in this chapter, are of value to all men regardless of sexual preferences.

Pornography is a multi-million pound business. You will see it at every news-stand and it is one of the driving forces of the internet. No matter where you turn, you can find constant opportunities for men in particular to try to satisfy their sexual needs through pornography. Why? Who has created this demand for pornography? Is it a purely natural male instinct? Is it just the quenching of a thirst? Or is it something else that has grown out of modern man's insecurity and lack of self-knowledge and self-worth?

There seems little wrong for instance in the basic notion that we enjoy admiring beautiful things. Be it a beautiful woman or a work of art, we find our senses are pleased by such experiences. It is a completely natural instinct to want more of those things that please us.

It seems likely, however, that pornography itself rarely produces any type of lasting pleasure. Nor does it seem to engender feelings in the viewer of self-worth or value. If anything the reverse is true. Does a man who satisfies himself as a result of flicking through a hard core magazine or web site, really come away with a good feeling about himself? Is it more that he did what he thought had to be done, that he had no choice? It wasn't what he ideally would have wanted, but at least he felt the relief of an orgasm.

An itch that had to be scratched. And this is the way that we have been encouraged to scratch our itches. Away from others, behind closed doors in secret dens and lairs. After all, what messages have we been given by our parents, school teachers and other influential figures about sexuality and desire?

Today, sex education has become an established part of the school curriculum. The workings of the body and the use of contraceptives are being explained to a younger and younger audience. Years ago, men and women were told very little. In most cases you found out the information for yourself – gathering snippets from overheard conversations and magazine articles.

The need for physical explanations in this education is great and it is good to see schools informing children. However, the need for information about the value of feelings and how to handle relationships is equally great. The lack of this type of information in our education may well have helped to contribute to the fragmentation that exists within many relationships today.

For many of us in our youth, teachings on the workings of the body, let alone feelings and sexual desires, were non-existent. And what did that lack of discussion produce in most of us men? A thought that our sexuality is not something to be proud of, not something to be discussed generally, and probably something to be feared.

There is no doubt that men and women find certain subjects difficult to discuss. Mothers have found it easier to explain to their daughters the mechanics and workings of the female body as well as accompanying emotional developments, and this has naturally given mother and daughter a closer connection. Quite understandably however, mothers have been reticent to discuss with their sons the feelings of desire, love and lust that they may be experiencing. After all, mother is not a man. And father? How many of us have experienced honest and open communication about sexual and emotional feelings with our fathers?

IAN

Ian was 13 years old when he first started to notice an unusual feeling rising through his body. This feeling seemed to coincide with seeing the same girl who went past his house every morning. His heart would start racing, he could feel himself blushing – even though no-one was ever watching him – and inside his trousers something seemed to be stirring.

One day at school, he hears his mates talking about 'wanking'. Interpreting this as a way of experiencing physically this wonderful feeling he has when he sees this girl, he listens closely, pretending to know exactly what they are talking about of course. He sees one of them with an adult magazine and asks if he can borrow it. Later that day, before his mum and dad return home, he steps into the bathroom with the magazine and, as written about in one of the magazine stories, he 'shoots his first load'.

The physical experience shocks him. It was not what he expected somehow. His heart felt little, although there was no doubt his body experienced something powerful.

Thinking he must be doing something wrong Ian tries again. And again. And again. He is soon addicted to the physical experience, stealing into the bathroom at every opportunity whenever he thinks his mum and dad won't notice (which they do of course, but they just don't know how to handle it).

Something continues to be missing. There is no connection between his heart and his penis. Since the penis seems to be working, he unconsciously blames the heart. As the man develops inside the boy, Ian becomes cold and emotionless. A sense of guilt also grows. The love impulse becomes quite separate from the erotic impulse. He gets into relationships in life which seem to be living proof that 'men are only after one thing'. And why? Was it because the pictures couldn't love him back?

Even when relationships have started, some men still find that pornography goes on to influence their lives. Here they are with their own physical partner and yet still finding themselves using the same magazines that they used when they were single. The initial desire to express themselves sexually has turned into a habit which some may now find difficult to do without. This can create an extra millstone around their necks within a loving relationship, because they feel it is something that their partners may not understand.

It could be that men are scared of admitting what we find attractive and erotic because we have always been encouraged to keep these feelings to ourselves. It could also be that this fear has helped us to establish the 'under-the-counter' world of X-rated movies, magazines and the rest. A world where we can hide ourselves and attempt to meet our apparently unsocial physical needs. We have found that one way to retain our control whilst satisfying our lust, albeit often unsatisfactorily, is by resorting to the creation and use of pornography. Is it not time that we changed this distorted view of our needs?

A lack of information during crucial periods of our development into men has also led some men to the conclusion that sex is apparently something that we can have control over, as and when we want it, without recourse to a third party. It is no surprise that, by the time we enter into relationships, some of us already have a view formed of the opposite sex that indicates sexual pleasure should be a very important part of the various things they can do for us, when we want them to.

A Better Way To Love...

There are many ways in which we can bring about change. The most important of which is helping sex to become a subject which is no longer taboo, either for ourselves, or within the context of a relationship. We can help to bring about even greater change in the future as well by enabling our children to understand more of the 'feeling' side to a relationship. By discussing with them the subjects of love and respect, as well as the physical workings of the body, we could help them to grow into adults who will look for much more than just mechanical excellence in their relation-ships to come.

No-one can teach this role as well as a child's parents. If the child can witness wholeness and openness at home, and if mum **and** dad could find it within themselves to discuss their feelings and experience as appropriate to the age of the child, surely that child will benefit enormously.

To make this sort of communication possible in the future with our children, as men we first need to find out who we are. We need to find out what our sexuality means to us. We need to find out what our feelings tell us about real sexual joy. We need to appreciate the differences between how a man views sex and how a woman views sex. We need to learn to feel the difference between physical gratification and heart-felt joy. We need to feel the difference between lust and love. For the difference is enormous.

To begin to understand these differences, you need to find out more about yourself. You need to see where it is that you fit into the sexual relationships that you have at the moment – either with a partner or yourself.

Are you the provider? Are you the taker? Are you someone who feels uncertain about your own power and therefore just waits to be asked? Do you generally **have sex**, or are you able to **make love**? The difference is vast. Is sexual intercourse something you always have to get on with, or something that you are able to be patient with, listening equally to your partner's needs and giving in an unhurried and complete way?

It is how you feel about the answers to these questions that will begin to tell you a lot about where you are sexually. Are you happy being the provider always or the taker? Would you like to feel more powerful? Do you listen to each other and give freely?

Whatever the answers to these questions, you will almost certainly find that even more open and honest communication with yourself and your partner about your own sexual desires and needs will have an uplifting effect on your relationship. This is where respect and honesty merge together to help form a relationship based on unconditional love.

If you are not in a relationship it is still important to validate your own sexual needs and desires and not to judge them as being bad or dirty. Learning to nurture your feelings, giving them the time and value they deserve, is a big step towards learning to like who you are.

In practical terms, this can be done by setting aside a special place and time for you to celebrate your sexuality. Take the phone off the hook, put on good music, light some candles – create an atmosphere and setting in which you are giving your sexual energy the environment it deserves. Don't be tempted to hurry things – enjoy the journey as much as the destination.

Creating such a space will do much to enhance the joy you receive from any sexual act and will also reduce feelings of low self-esteem and guilt that often result from putting on a dirty movie and having an orgasm. If you subsequently become involved in a relationship, this ability to engage fully in the process will help to create greatly enhanced love-making.

If you are already in a relationship, by becoming more open and stating both your fantasies and your problems you are inviting someone into your heart. Don't expect your partner to fix your problems, or comply with your fantasies.

You may be into S&M, your partner may not even like being touched. The thought of sharing your truth may be frightening. But if you don't attempt to reveal the real you, you can be guaranteed that a void will always exist in your relationship. If you are prepared to share – the idea of which can be frightening – you will bridge the gap between you. This new openness allows a relationship to evolve in a way which enhances it, both physically and emotionally. It is from such a base that you can experience sex at a whole new level of enjoyment – even with the partner you have had for years!

Sexual desire is a natural instinct. The point to remember is that it takes on a very different meaning within the context of a loving relationship – whether that relationship is with yourself or another person. Sex becomes a tool of love, not the reason for the relationship.

MY LAST PROSTITUTE

As a young boy, I was always roaming the streets of Lyon, my hometown in France. The red light district was only a few miles from my house right in the centre of the city. Prostitution was legal there, and whores on sidewalks awaited customers, displaying as much of their flesh as allowed by law. To me, they all looked beautiful and erotic.

At twelve, my groin was already steaming at the sight of these luscious ladies. Regularly, I would swing by the district to have a look. I was fascinated. I would often pretend to be window-shopping in order to have a longer stare at them. As I walked by them, I would often say, "Hi." Getting close to them was absolutely the best. Even their smell I can still remember. Their world to me was something I wanted, their legs I longed to touch, and their breasts looked so warm and open. Their mysterious and ritualistic world was something I wanted to fathom.

One time – I was probably fourteen – I went inside one of the dark buildings where I knew some prostitutes worked, climbing four or five floors listening at every door for sounds. With all my innocence, I was searching for clues about sex in that somber world.

At home, there was never any talk about sex, except when my older brother, then in his early twenties, would tell me privately about his kinky sexual prowess. Sex was still a mystery. My attempts to conquer girls at school were quite unsuccessful. Then at the age of fifteen, at a friend's party, I was introduced to a hard-core porn magazine from Sweden. For the first time I saw how women's and men's genitals (as well as numerous other parts) fit together.

Staring at these images, the effect on me was like a hard drug. I was hooked! I had lost my innocence, and these images were carved into my psyche. I came across similar pictures in my brother's bedroom, and secretly looked at them when he was gone. For years such images haunted me.

After that, my taste for masturbation increased and so did my appetite for pornography. My twenties were a disaster sexually, even though my first sexual experience at eighteen was sweet and powerful. My addictions to pornographic images clashed with the reality of sex, with all its imperfections, emotions and inconveniences.

On a visit to my hometown – I must have been 25 – walking alone near the red lantern district, my groin got the best of me, and I went with my first prostitute. Her apartment was small, with a single bed. She washed my penis like a mother would do with her child. She asked me what I wanted. A blow job was my fancy. She asked me if I usually came quick. She proceeded with great skill and asked me if I also wanted to have intercourse. I declined, I was way too nervous. My ten bucks then, bought about three minutes of pleasure.

For the next ten years, I had many other encounters with prostitutes, in the US and abroad. I always got blow jobs. Whatever city I went to, I somehow always found them, as if magnetized to them. In 1988, I was traveling through Lisbon, Portugal. On the way back to my hotel from a night of drinking and listening to Fado music, I came across three prostitutes a couple of blocks from my hotel. I knew they were there for me. I talked to one of them and followed her into her building.

Her room was also small but with a large bed. She was very plain, in her early forties. She too washed me very carefully, giggling as we could not converse. She knew "fuck" in English, and I knew "obrigado" – thank you – in Portuguese. It made for poor conversational material!

She was sweet like a mother, and even seemed to enjoy giving me oral sex. Drunk as I was, I could barely keep it up. I left without having an orgasm.

The next night, coming back from another round of drinking, I took that same street, and there she was, as if waiting for me. She greeted me with a smile. She was so real and innocent-looking. For the first time with a prostitute, I wanted to have intercourse. I took her from behind. Nervous and drunk, I wasn't very gentle and seemed to hurt her.

The pain I saw on her beautiful face made me stop. It was as if a train had hit me. I put my pants back on, kissed her on the cheeks and left for my hotel.

I felt incredibly ashamed, sorry and sad. For the first time in ten years, after having been with many prostitutes, I was suddenly being honest with myself, acknowledging how lost I truly was, how addicted I was. I wrote profusely in my journal that night, as if laying out a confession. And I made a commitment to stop this habit. It became clear how these addictions and patterns were affecting my ability to be intimate and sexually fulfilled with my lovers.

Since then, much healing has taken place. I've had to be extremely committed and disciplined, just like any addict in recovery. Slowly, the magical and sacred world of sexuality has revealed its face, overshadowing the rubble of my pornographic past. Looking back at my youth, I wish that, at home or at school, sexuality could have been addressed in a wholesome, joyous, and simple way. Instead the vacuum got filled with what was cheap and readily available.

I never knew any of these ladies' names. I remember some of their faces. I am grateful to the woman of Lisbon. She was my last prostitute.

The female and male bodies are beautiful forms, both of which have the ability to stimulate men. To keep what things we find stimulating to ourselves, prevents our partner from being able to join us in that experience of love and pleasure. This has to blunt the excitement and joy that a relationship can gain from understanding more fully each other's sexual desires and preferences.

Instead of using pornography as a vehicle through which we are able to let off steam sexually, let us look to partners for help and support in enabling us to blossom sexually. Let us share our feelings, desires and urges with another who cares for us. And in that sharing let us discover a whole new level of enjoyment and pleasure that will put into perspective the difference between enjoyment of the part and enjoyment of the whole.

Let us discuss our worries and problems together; let us view beautiful images together; let us share erotic tales and fantasies together. But let us view in love; let us share in love; let us love in joy. Let us unite ourselves through our sharing and thereby free ourselves to welcome in a whole new dawn in male sexuality.

PHILLIP

Phillip had grown up feeling great uncertainty about his own sexuality, an uncertainty that had been fuelled by uncommunicative parents and an education which had completely fudged the subject of sex. By the time he had reached his mid twenties he had experienced nothing but a series of meaningless one-night stands and failed short term relationships.

The pornography that he had latched onto during his

teenage years had followed him through into adult life. Once he had connected to the internet, hard core sites became easy to access and his behaviour grew into a loveless, time-consuming, money-wasting and morale-sapping addiction.

To his own great surprise however, he started a new relationship. A relationship that somehow seemed different from the rest, although he couldn't say why. And soon he found himself engaged and not long after that he was married.

One day his wife walked in while he was on the internet and caught him looking at some hard core pornography. Far from being furious with him (as he had feared) – she found herself quite turned on by the idea that there was more to his sexuality than she had so far discovered. She wasn't too keen on the pictures he was looking at, but she was intrigued to know what her husband fantasised about.

They started talking about their sexual desires and fantasies and, whilst they didn't exactly share similar dreams, they soon learnt to allow each other to have their own.

In this atmosphere of openness (which had been instigated by his wife), Phillip began to feel less apprehensive in the bedroom. Sex started to improve dramatically for both of them. As their knowledge of each other increased, so Phillip found himself able to satisfy his wife in ways that they had never dreamt of as being possible. This increased awareness spilt over into their daily lives as they established a deeper level of understanding and empathy within their relationship. Emotionally they became much closer and this increased feeling of security created a far greater sense of self-worth in Phillip.

As Phillip's self-esteem grew, so did his love life; his wife started to pleasure him in ways that had not been possible before, for she had had no idea what he wanted. Now she found herself able to bring a whole new dimension of enjoyment into his life, just by understanding a little more about him.

As their sexuality as a partnership developed, so Phillip's dependency upon pornography diminished. It didn't happen overnight, but it did happen. Exploring and adventuring with another human being, albeit with certain limitations, was so much more rewarding than the passionless study of celluloid sex.

Eighteen months or so after his wife first strayed into his office at home and discovered his secret, Phillip found himself out in his back garden holding a lighted match. In front of him lay a pile of magazines, some of them ten years old; as the match set the first chewed corner alight, Phillip knew that he had finally traded lust for love.

Checklist:-

1) If someone took away all the pornography in the world, could you still get stimulated? Don't be tempted to use pornography to avoid your own inner search for emotional love.

2) Come out! Talk to your partner about sex and love openly. Remember each time you share your truth with someone you **empower** yourself and them.

3) Review your role. Are you always giving, or always taking? Look to create some balance.

4) Anything that helps to deepen your relationship with your partner will help to enhance your sexual experiences. Be honest with yourself and each other.

5) Give yourself the time and an uplifting environment in which to celebrate your own sexual needs – whether with a partner or by yourself. Just because you may be alone, does not mean you need to devalue or hurry your experiences.

8

Creating Time

"...time the devourer of everything"

Ovid

Ask most men what they would like more of and if the answer isn't sex or money – it will be time. None of us seems to have enough. And it also seems that no-one is responsible for this. It is just how the world is. It is just how things are. It is just how things must be.

"Sorry darling, I've got to be here for a meeting", "I must dash, Mum, doctor's appointment", "Sorry kids no time to play, got to check my e-mail". Where will it end? As it is we deprive ourselves of all sorts of vital daily things because of our need to hurry. Love, food, sleep, conversation – all things that we curtail or postpone or cancel because of our need to meet deadlines. And yet who are we meeting these deadlines for? The answers come back thick and fast. My boss, my colleagues, my partner. Well when are we going to start meeting deadlines that **we** set?

Are we really listening to our own needs often enough? Do we really need to live life at this breakneck speed all the time, or is it purely habit? How many of us for instance find that we work and work and work leading up to our holiday, only to find that when we finally switch off and slow down we have developed flu, if not something worse? How many of us find that when we ask the children to do something for us, we expect them to do it for us right this minute, even though they may be involved in some other game or activity?

NICK

Nick was married with children and, although he had been a university lecturer, his lack of confidence had led him into a job as a cab driver. His low self-esteem had established a pattern in his life where he was always doing things for others. He could never say no, whether it was his boss asking him to do overtime, or a friend suddenly needing a hand. This understandably often led him into clashes with his wife who was also desperate for his time. Whatever he did, it seemed he couldn't do the right thing.

Nick frequently complained about not having enough time to do anything and became a victim of this misunderstanding of time. His children became distant and his wife gave up hoping that she would ever have him around to support her.

Life went downhill. His hatred of his job and lack of satisfaction in life left him feeling completely demoralised. When asked why he didn't try to get a job in his old profession, he replied : "I've got all these things to do – I haven't got time to attend interviews".

(continued...)

So manic have we become that our whole life tends to revolve around schedules. Schedules that very often we are merely playing a part in rather than taking hold of and saying "Hey, hang on a second, this is my life, I want to have a say in what happens and when". We may have come so far down this path, that most of us no longer realise that we have any say in how our time is filled.

I would suggest that nothing could be further from the truth.

Our time is our own. Our life is our own. Only we ourselves can make our decisions. Believe it or not, we have chosen our schedules as they exist at the moment and only we can choose to change them.

If you are the sort of man who is frequently hurrying and

never seems to have enough time for anything, then now is the time to consider change. Change your approach to yourself, start taking your own needs and desires more seriously and you may find that you begin to abandon activities which no longer fit in with who you now wish to be. You may well find yourself with **more** time on your hands. The more time you spend listening to your own requirements, the more time you will have to fulfil them. Carry on hurrying from place to place, from meeting to meeting, from TV programme to TV programme and you will find you will never have enough time to do all the things that you really want.

There is a saying in the financial world that you have to 'speculate to accumulate'. The same is true of time. If you spend more time listening to your own needs, you are likely to accumulate more time to do these things.

There is no reason to be proud of the fact that we are always busy. We could all fill our time permanently. Part of the reward that we may receive from this hectic activity is that it makes us feel important, it makes us feel wanted. Having to be somewhere all the time not only gives us a feeling of importance and value in society, but it also gives us 'valid' reasons as to why we cannot attend to this family matter or that relationship problem. Time spent at work becomes in particular a fact of life which apparently can't be controlled. We have become pawns in a game that, judging by the state of some men today, we are not sure we even enjoy playing that much.

The key question is not how much of my time do I fill every day, but **how much of my time do I fill doing what I love?**

Here we are often complaining of not having enough time, only to find that we spend much of our time doing things that we don't really enjoy. People talk about quality time as if time itself were the problem. It is not. And it never can be. The conditioning that tells us to fill every available minute is the problem and that can only change if we choose to change it. No amount of complaining about the lack of time will make one bit of difference. We have to change our understanding of our relationship to time if we are to start making the best use of the time that we have.

Changing our view of time can have extraordinary effects upon our lives. If we can start to change from feeling we have to get things done as quickly as possible to wanting to do something that is as good as we could do, we will find that our end result is that much better and consequently our self-esteem that much higher. For instance, explaining to a client that we think their deadline is going to jeopardise the end result can only make us feel better about ourselves, even if we end up losing that job. This generally doesn't happen. Worthwhile businesses would far rather employ conscientious people with high standards.

It is the feeling that we have somehow achieved something good that is so important in our development as men. Getting things done quickly is unlikely to engender the same positive feeling. It is perhaps through this greater understanding of our relationship to time that we could begin to contribute so much more to improving the environment that we live in.

NICK (...continued)

When I first started to work with Nick, he was very down. It was clear that his low self-esteem was combining with this warped view of time to make life extremely difficult.

I introduced him to another view of time. I suggested that time was something over which he had control; that time was something that he had to spend according to how he most wanted to; that time was one of the most precious gifts he would ever be given and wasn't it now worth using that gift wisely.

Taking very small steps Nick started to change his understanding of his relationship to time. His first move was to start thinking of it as something that he could choose to use in whatever way he felt would help him best. He became the priority; not others; not time. Nick.

Seeing himself as the leading figure in this game enabled

him to admit that what he really wanted was to resume lecturing. He was encouraged to start spending some of his time imagining himself finding the perfect job advertisement. Within a short time, an advert appeared.

"But my boss will never give me the time off for the interview", he stated in despair, having shown me the ad. I encouraged him further to follow his emotions, which were clearly encouraging him to apply for the job. This I did very simply by use of 'the Magic Wand' technique...

We all have magic wands and they are very simple to use! You just state a question in your head that you would like guidance on (e.g. "I want to know whether to change careers?"). You then 'wave the magic wand' by imagining various different outcomes or answers to the question you have raised (e.g. "I have now changed careers and am preparing for my first day at work" or "Six months have passed and I am still in my old job").

You will invariably find that one potential outcome will give you a much better feeling than anything else. This feeling, which you can recognise by a sense of joy or lightness, represents an inner truth that will never disappoint you if you pay attention to it.

... With Nick I 'waved the magic wand' and asked him to imagine giving up on the idea of his changing career, thus remaining as a cab driver. He said that felt very heavy to him. I then waved it again and asked him to imagine resuming lecturing. Immediately his face lightened and a smile crept across it from one ear to the other. It felt much better. I suggested that this was his truth and that if he followed it he would be given what he needed to fulfil this truth.

I suggested that if the job was meant to be then the time required for the interview would be made available for him. I asked him to consider writing a letter to his boss requesting the time off (his confidence was far too low to ask his boss directly at this stage).

Much to Nick's amazement the time was granted. Not only that, but he got the job. The last time I spoke to him, some two years after his career change, he had become firmly established in his job. He added that, whilst he said he was still prone to slipping into old habits occasionally, his change of perspective on time had had a very positive effect on many other areas of his life. He also gets his magic wand out from time to time...

Checklist:-

1) Ask yourself who is setting your deadlines – you, or somebody else? If it's somebody else, it's time you took back control of your life. This is your time we're talking about, no-one else's.

2) Spend a little more time listening to yourself and a little less time doing. Learn just to "be". You are after all a human **being** not a human **doing**.

3) Don't seek to be busy all the time (that is not a real sign of success). Aim to fill a little of your time with more frivolous things that are fun. You may be surprised at what they lead to.

4) Do things to the best of your ability – don't be tempted to compromise your own high standards for a deadline that can probably be shifted anyway.

5) If you are struggling with a difficult decision or situation, get all the help you can from inside as well as outside. State the question or problem in your head, 'wave the magic wand' by imagining various different outcomes/solutions, and see if you get a better feeling about one specific approach. Pay attention

to the answer that gives you a really good feeling. If nothing does, then it just means you are not clear yet. Allow things to become clearer before taking action. You have all the time in the world!

6) It is not time that is your enemy, it is your understanding of your relationship to it.

9

Addictive Behaviour

"...I have very poor and unhappy brains for drinking:
I could well wish courtesy would invent
some other custom of entertainment."

William Shakespeare

Alcohol, drugs, gambling, sex, cigarettes – we've got plenty of things on which we can put the blame for our own lack of health and happiness. It is fairly easy to say that an addiction is to blame for certain flaws in our character. It is equally easy to claim that we have no control over them and that we're just a victim of something evil that someone else has invented. It's also easy to say that we don't have a drink, drug or cigarette problem and then spend the next few weeks proving quite the opposite to those people who witness our behaviour every day – normally our closest friends and family.

It is interesting how many men will go to a therapist or counsellor and state quite clearly that they don't have a problem with any of these addictions. Very often their partner or work colleagues have coerced them into seeking help. And yet one would think that if these things were bringing any problems in to his life, the man in question would want to try to stop the habit or addiction.

MARTIN

Martin and Susan had been married for 26 years. Their marriage had been difficult from the start, as it soon became apparent to Susan that Martin had alcohol problems. She soon found herself pregnant and a couple of years after their first child was born another was on the way.

Motherhood distracted Susan from addressing the problem in her marriage. Martin continued to drink, generally falling asleep in his chair and not making it up to bed before three or four in the morning. Sex became sporadic and indifferent, generally for Susan it became an occasional extra burden prior to getting to sleep.

By the time the children were ready to leave home many years later, Susan felt she was ready to help Martin address his problem. Martin's response was predictable, he didn't think he had a problem, but he agreed to seek counselling with his wife for the sake of their marriage.

But when push came to shove, Martin just couldn't own up to a problem. Different counsellors tried to help them, but each had to concede to Martin's continual insistence that his drinking was not a problem for him. Susan gave up hope that there was any more she could do to help and, in spite of Martin's 'desire' to help save the marriage, is currently seeking legal advice.

So why is it that we are sometimes so loath to attempt to fix something that we know is quite often detrimental to our health and happiness? Is it our lack of determination? Is it our belief that it's a hopeless addiction over which we have no control? Is it our pride that makes us refuse to be told by anyone else what is and what is not good for us? Or is it that we have become so cut off from our feelings, from who we really are, that we find it difficult to recognise when we're experiencing a problem?

Certainly the last suggestion contains a great element of truth for many of us. An example of this is work. Many men are addicted to work, although few may admit to it. It is seen throughout society as a beneficial or acceptable addiction. But no addiction can be beneficial – addiction implies imbalance, not balance. Look at the amount of time you spend commuting to work, at work, thinking about work. What percentage of your time awake is spent on work in one form or another? Now think about how much time you give the rest of your life – your home life, your family and your fun. Work it out and write it down. Study the figures. Do you have balance?

Another possible root of our failure to want to remove 'addictions' in our life could be our lack of belief that we are worthy of anything better. That somehow we deserve to self-destruct and so we are merely giving ourselves what we are worth.

I believe that one of the problems with addictive behaviour of any sort is not the addiction itself, but the collective lack of self-esteem that males in particular have inherited. I would suggest that at a deep level we do not feel valued, we often feel like failures and we often believe that others don't really want to hear our true opinions or see the real us. Consequently we hide ourselves in addictions and self-destruct in a way that seems to give us a limited amount of pleasure.

For instance it is interesting to note the time at which some addictions are triggered. Often these addictions will not be a problem when we are genuinely stimulated by an activity – immersed in our favourite hobby for instance or taking part in a fascinating meeting.

These 'desires' may well float into consciousness when we are bored. When all of a sudden we are faced with the prospect of our own silence, or of company that does not stimulate us, it could be that we look for things in which we can lose ourselves. Activities that may help us to ignore the one thing – our inner guidance – that could really help us to improve our position, and help us to avoid these unwanted situations in the future .

It is possible that we have become so scared of our emotions, our inner voice, that we will do almost anything to drown them out. Maybe we fear that once these emotions start to pour out, they will never stop. We must remember that, as children, we have been taught very specifically not to feel ("stop crying child", "don't lose your temper", "don't get so excited"). As we grow up we find that to contain the build-up of these feelings we have to resort to stronger and stronger means. Addictions become established.

Drinking, smoking, news watching, working to excess – in fact any form of addictive behaviour – can prevent us from having to listen to the voice of our emotions. One is no better or more dangerous than the other. They are all tools that help us ignore the inner guidance we would receive if we only sat still for long enough to listen.

Many people attempt to give up bad habits and addictions, and then find they have gone back to them within a few days, weeks or months. In the same way that someone can be free of cancer for many years, only for it to return at a later date and out of the blue, so a former addiction can return, even after years. Why?

Is it because the cause itself has not been dealt with?

Taking Control Of Addictions

We have advanced in many ways in our understanding of the physical reasons for addictive behaviour but do we really understand causes? Do we really understand fully the part that we may be playing in our addiction?

I believe that we live in a world where we have free will. A place where we can choose to say, do or believe in whatever we want to. This applies to both men and women. I further believe that we have chosen every aspect of our lives as they exist at present, and we are continuing to choose our future through our thoughts as they exist now. No-one is making us smoke or drink or work constantly. We are choosing to do these things. For many of us this may well be difficult to accept.

However, if we can accept that there is no-one outside ourselves standing over us insisting that we drink or smoke, then we must further accept that this message must be coming from inside us. If it is coming from inside us then doesn't it make sense to try to find out what that voice is really trying to tell us, what our need for a certain thing may really be telling us about ourselves?

It seems possible that an addiction may be an imbalance in the same way that illness is. It is also possible that, through the recognition and curing of the addiction, some sort of inner voice may be trying to get a message across to the man involved. A message which may well contain vital information in helping that man to achieve his own highest potential.

For this reason, I would never recommend just trying to break the habit (for example, by throwing away all your cigarettes immediately). That could be to ignore the message and certainly will not deal with the cause of the problem. There has to be a real desire to overcome an addiction, and that desire is most powerful if it represents a very positive thought. Have perfect health as a goal for instance, and it seems clear that chain-smoking or heavy drinking are unlikely to feature in the pursuit of such an aim. Don't focus on the need to stop your addiction. Focus on what you are wanting to create. Instead of coming from a negative place, you will be coming from a very positive one.

Stopping for the sake of stopping will never last. Stopping because of fear will produce similar results. When we decide that we want to change something in our lives, we have to start looking at the positive reasons for bringing about the change. Remember, like attracts like, and if we try to do something from a negative base (for example – "I must stop smoking or else I'll get cancer") then we are likely to attract more negative experiences to us. If instead we start from a positive base ("I want to become healthier and fitter") then we will attract the positive experience to us.

Try not to fall into the trap of time either by saying that you must break this habit by such and such a date. Think about the man that you want to change into and allow the habit or addiction to change as you do. No great effort, no personal torture; just firm, continuous clarity of who you want to be – a man with purpose and focus who is tied to nothing and therefore free.

JOHN

John had an alcohol problem and had attempted suicide on two occasions. He could think of no reason to live at all. He was encouraged to write down all his fears and, although he found this quite difficult to start with, he soon had a list of fifteen fears. These fears included drinking himself into oblivion and losing the respect of his family.

John was then shown how to turn these fears into things that

he would like to have happen. "I fear losing the respect of my family" turned into "I want to earn my family's respect"; "I fear drinking myself into oblivion" became "I want to be in control of my desire for alcohol".

Before long, someone who a few minutes previously could think of no reason to live, now found himself with fifteen powerful reasons for living. And yet nothing in his physical life had changed. It was just a change of perspective.

This simple clarity helped him to think of some practical things he could do to create change, one of which was offering to mow an elderly relation's lawn. He had never done this in his life before. His offer of help was gratefully received and his action helped him to feel that he was already on his way to achieving one of his most desired goals – earning his family's respect.

Checklist:-

1) Don't underestimate how difficult it is to be honest with yourself about any addictions you have in your life. But remember, once you've owned up to the problem, you could be well on the way towards fixing it.

2) Addiction to work is still an addiction. It needs to be balanced with the rest of your life. How balanced is the work in your life?

3) Don't let your addiction drown out your inner voice. Learn to listen inwardly and benefit from the help you will receive through your emotions.

4) Breaking addictions can be sustainable if you start from a positive place. Imagine what you want in life, feel the power of those thoughts coming true and start looking for ways to make those things come true. Don't be tempted into focusing on your need to stop doing something. Always look to create.

5) Never put deadlines on quitting addictions. Let them work their way out naturally, dying down like a fire. Keep reminding yourself what you want out of life.

10

Letting Go Of Attachments

"...fool, not to know that love endures no tie."

John Dryden

THE IRON BARON

When the ship 'Iron Baron' sank in Hobart, Australia, one of the crew was so afraid of drowning that he clung to the rails of the sinking ship and could not be rescued. He drowned, while his shipmates were saved.

This chapter is about attachments; the things that – like the ship the sailor clung to in the story above – we often cling to fiercely even though they are capable of bringing us great harm.

Attachment To Our Own Point Of View

Having a fixed view on anything may well be damaging. Men who are unwilling to listen to others' points of view because of their belief that their own standpoint is unchangeable will often run into confrontation.

In moments of stress it is not at all uncommon for a man to be unwilling even to consider that someone else may have a point of view or a suggestion which may also be of benefit. So why is it that once a man 'believes' in one approach to life, he is often so unwilling to believe in another, another which may not even be contrary to his own, but just slightly different?

Our desire to show that we are right is often the cause of this stubbornness. Unfortunately it also results in our remaining closed to ideas or information which may be of great use to us. What we would do well to remember is that not one of us has a monopoly on being right. There is not a man alive today who could possibly have all the answers to everything. We have each other so that we can learn from each other, not in order that we can see who can shout the loudest. And yet trying to shout the loudest is so often what we find ourselves doing, particularly when something sensitive or challenging is being raised.

Understandably, many of us use our own 'points of view' and 'principles' to defend our position, even to hide our ignorance of a particular subject. This often results in the theme of a 'threatening' conversation (that is, a conversation that may challenge our beliefs and knowledge) being converted into something that we then feel more confident to discuss. Having changed the subject matter, albeit sometimes in a very subtle way, we are then able to rattle off our usual 'speech' and convince the other party or parties that they have no choice but to agree. Having won back the discussion, our desire to stamp our authority on the conversation often results in a very different subject from the original theme being discussed.

Other people who take part in such conversations will recognise the feeling of coming away from a conversation confused and dissatisfied with its outcome. In this instance the male 'aggressor', having 'proved' his point, comes away with his beliefs further reinforced by the inability of the others to dispute his standpoint and fails to see entirely that it is he who has missed the point.

So what can we learn from this common scenario? We can observe that fear of confrontation, of having views challenged, may often prevent real sharing from taking place. We can also learn that many men have a need to be dominant which may often be counter-productive. We would all, always, like to be thought of as being right. We would all like to be considered wise. But where does wisdom really lie? In the person who shouts loudest, or the one who listens closest?

THE WISDOM OF YOUTH

I was sitting having a chat with Den, the young man mentioned in chapter three of this book. In the couple of months we had been meeting he had begun to feel better and was beginning to find purpose in his life. A more relaxed, balanced and positive state of mind had resulted in drastically reduced medication which, in itself, had improved his general level of well-being.

Half way through a conversation on attachment to a point of view, he made the following statement:

"Barry, the way I see it, we were born with two ears and one mouth. So I reckon that if I listen twice as much as I talk in life, I'll probably do okay."

So simple and yet so true. It seems we may be scared of listening to others, because we don't want to admit to ourselves that there are things we don't understand. We are scared of ideas that might not fit in with our firm beliefs about the world. We are scared of admitting to others that well, this isn't really my belief, it's something my Dad told me or that I read in a book. We are scared of having to admit to ourselves that in fact many of the things we hold rigidly to may be words and ideas that others have presented to us. They may not be things that we 'feel' to be the truth. We may have just made them ours because it has helped us to form our own identity. Without such ideas, we fear that our identity itself would be threatened. It may well be that we now need to give ourselves permission to reconsider some of those limiting beliefs.

Our true identity, our true self, can only really be formed out of **our own feelings**. Out of our own experiences and our appreciation of those experiences. Nobody else's dogma, beliefs, experiences can give us an identity. It has to come from within. And the only way it can come from within is if we allow ourselves to listen. Essentially, to listen to ourselves; but also to listen to other people's points of view and accounts of their experiences so that we may decide for ourselves what **feels** good and what **feels** bad.

To tell someone they are crazy just because they have a certain belief is foolish. That person's belief may be the very thing that brings them happiness every day. Who are we to judge that as being wrong? We do not have to agree with what anyone else says or does or feels, but we must at least accept it as being their experience.

The following is a good example of why it is so important to allow ourselves and others to express truths without judgment:

The Painters

You are sitting in a large room with five hundred other people. You are all staring at a large painting on a wall which you have been asked to study for a few minutes. Carefully, you study the image, trying to pick up on all the different aspects that are represented.

After a few minutes you are all then asked to go into the next room where you are given paints and a piece of paper. "Paint the painting you have just been studying," requests the facilitator. You work hard to get down on paper as much about the picture as you can remember. After much effort, you are asked to put down your paintbrushes and to go round the room comparing pictures.

And what do you find? Five hundred and one completely different versions of the painting. Of course some of them have similar bits, but no two paintings in the room are the same.

"Each of us can understand" starts the facilitator "that everyone here has expressed their version of the truth. And yet no two versions are the same. Now you could try and convince anyone else in here that their painting is wrong, that they have got the colour of the sky wrong, or the shape of the tree. But to do so would be futile. Each one of you has painted what you felt to be the truth at that time. No-one has lied. No-one has bent the truth. Each person has just expressed themselves honestly and no amount of cajoling can change that."

Everyone stops to consider the implications of what is being said. The facilitator continues: "How would it be if we applied this simple idea in our lives? Imagine if we let everyone express their own version of the truth in as non-judgmental way as we have done here this afternoon?"

The point is simply made. Feeling slightly embarrassed and hoping that no-one can read your mind, you start to think of all those times that you have tried to convince someone that they shouldn't feel a certain way. That somehow their truth was 'wrong'.

Maybe one of the reasons we dispute other people's feelings is because we feel threatened. Perhaps we fear that our wife/son/daughter/mother/colleague may consider themselves superior to us for having taught us something. We want other people to think that we have all the answers. But of course, we don't. And we never will. Surely we would learn so much more if we were able to remain open to what others have to teach us.

We would benefit greatly from letting go of any beliefs which limit us, whether they are religious ("Catholics/Christians/Buddhists etc. are fools" or "There is no God"), financial ("I'll always be hard up"), racial ("I hate Serbs/Whites/Blacks"), emotional ("I can't cry") or any other dogmatic thoughts or stances. If you are rigid and inflexible in your approach to life, the likelihood is that all around you you will observe rigid and inflexible people.

Be willing to listen, be willing to change even the strongest beliefs, and you may witness a world that is full of new beginnings and compassionate, helpful and interesting people.

Avoiding The Truth?

Sometimes room to breathe, away from work, away from families, away from anything to do with our regular routine is vital. We all need to be refreshed from time to time by new surroundings and experiences. Hard working family men will often be found taking single skiing holidays, sports tours, climbing expeditions, regular rounds of golf or trips to the pub. But, like so many other panaceas that we use to alleviate our pain, we often find that these short trips and escapes do little in the long term to sort out our frustration and unhappiness.

When we 'disappear' without our families, we may occasionally be carrying a lot more excess baggage with us than just our golf clubs or skis. Often we will go with our partner's full support. But other times we may well be abandoning partners who have worked tirelessly at child rearing/jobs/home throughout the year and whose resentment, spoken or not, travels with us wherever we go.

As we have already seen, men love to feel in control. We love to feel that by doing something, by taking some sort of physical action, we are bringing about a desired end result. When we feel shattered and drained as a result of the pressures of life, we feel we are helping to deal with those pressures by taking ourselves off for a few hours/days/ weeks to a place where we can do something we **really** love. We think that by so doing we will come back a better employee, husband, lover or father.

This is not always the case. We invariably come back to the same circumstances that we left. The same job; the same partner; the same children; the same problems. Time away can in fact end up disempowering us if it becomes the means through which we lose familiarity with our family, friends or colleagues.

What we need most is to use the perspective that we have gained as a result of a break to make changes in our life and to create deeper and better communication with those around us. Time away can easily **empower** us – but only if we choose to learn from what it teaches us about our lives.

Life As A Canvas

Think of life as a canvas on which you have already begun to fill in some details. Some of those details you like, others you don't like. But you are not sure which parts are wrong and which are right. So you decide to take a break from the canvas for a little while so that you can come back to it refreshed, with clearer vision.

A few hours/days/weeks later you return. The painting is exactly as you left it. But now you can see more clearly what you like about it and what you don't like. Are you prepared to make some changes?

Where A Partner Fits In

"But what about my partner? She gets together quite often with the girls over coffee and chats and stuff. I mean it's not exactly pressure." And indeed to many of us what our partner does, even if it involves work, may not appear to involve real pressure. But how do we measure pressure?

To many men, pressure is having to make a key business decision within a certain amount of time; having to finish a report and presentation and present it to the board; having to find the money to pay the mortgage or the time to get to the gym or the golf course.

Whilst many more women now also face these same pressures, many others face a quite different level of stress within the still commonplace domestic set-up. To a mother for instance, pressure may be having to think of something new to do with a screaming toddler to get through the remaining hours before Dad gets home; pressure may be having to remember to pick up the oldest child from school whilst coping with a sick infant and a heavy period; pressure may be having to decide whether to stimulate her own need for excitement again by returning to work at the cost of leaving her children with someone she doesn't know; pressure may be sacrificing her own intellectual, creative or emotional needs while she brings up the family, often with little support; pressure may be having to sound pleased that her partner is going to get the rest he so 'badly needs' by going off for a week with some male friends, leaving her alone to cope with the family.

And coping is often all that happens. We may be at the stage where if we 'cope' with our families we feel we are succeeding. And yet where is the joy in just coping? Is it really good enough for ourselves and our children? Do we really want to breed a generation of copers? An observation of cancer statistics would suggest that may be a very dangerous thing to do. Copers may be more likely to get cancer than people who fight for what they want and say no when they are not prepared to do something.

But it is perfectly possible that the pressure many men find themselves under every day is creating just this – a generation of copers. A generation of people who put up with being treated badly, who find themselves unable to deal with emotional issues and who therefore cope with life until such time as their needs demand to be heard.

When this pattern of behaviour starts surfacing in a man, it is a signal that he may need to do quite the reverse from abandoning his life for a few days in the hope that when he comes back things will have improved. He may well need to look more closely at his life to see how he is meeting his needs every day and where he may be able to make changes to ease that pressure. Time away can provide that clarity, so can time at home. What is certain is that merely 'escaping' is not the answer.

ANDY

Andy was married with two young boys. He had recently started working from home more often, in order to see more of his family. He had set up an office in their study and had told the boys they were never to interrupt him once he was 'at work'.

James and Tom were 4 and 2. They didn't understand work, and whilst they were obviously pleased that Daddy was around a little more now, they certainly didn't understand why they couldn't play with him all the time. And so time upon time, they would barge into his office and demand attention. Andy's partner did her best to divert them but knowing that Dad was there was just too much of a temptation for the little boys. One day, in despair, Andy locked the door. He would have been better off being at work than doing that. The children screamed and yelled until finally he relented. He couldn't work anyway with all that noise.

And then a peculiar thing happened. Andy, not knowing

what else he could do to distract them from their tears, sat down and started to play with them. That in itself wasn't unusual – he was always very good at playing with them outside of work. What was peculiar was this; he played for no more than about ten minutes and then, seeing that the boys seemed quite absorbed, he explained that he was just popping back to do a couple of things in his office. The boys continued playing. An hour went by and Andy managed to get what seemed like twice the work done that he would normally have achieved in the same time. And what's more, he felt really good about himself. He came back out of his office and the boys didn't even look up.

From that point on Andy and his partner have practised the same approach. A few minutes of attention, validation that their desire for Daddy is very much understood and the boys then let Daddy go and do the things that Daddy needs to do. Some days he needs to give them more time, other days they need less. They have learnt to respect each other's needs and are all bene-fitting as a result.

We have inherited a set of beliefs that include the suggestion that our happiness lies in 'shutting the door' on our problems. That idea may have been useful for one generation, but does it serve men well today? I don't believe it does. I believe that the very people from whom we are often escaping are the very people whom, if we got to know better, would have some of the answers we need to help us create greater joy and pleasure.

It's important to have your trips and time to yourself, but try to avoid using them as a way of keeping bearable a situation that you need to roll up your sleeves and fix.

Telephones, Faxes and Emails

DAVID

David had worked for his company for eleven years, giving them some of the best years of his life and being rewarded well in return. He had built up many good friendships within the firm and had generally enjoyed himself.

Then one day they were bought out by an American firm. Everyone was assured at the time that they were not to worry, but David couldn't help feeling that something was going to happen.

Soon after the take-over, one Friday afternoon, David and all the other staff received a memo. The memo requested all employees to be in and by their phone the following Monday between 8.30am and 10.00am. David suspected the worst.

He spent the week-end as best he could. However, on the

Monday morning he arrived at his desk shattered from lack of sleep and worry. The office felt like an abattoir. It didn't help when his phone kept ringing with clients. Each time it went he could feel his adrenalin pumping.

When it rang at 9.27am, David had had so many calls he was beginning to forget the significance of the phone that morning. That was until an unfamiliar, cold voice told him he was 'surplus to requirements'. Years of effort, of heart-break and happiness, of panics and clinched deals, of all-night negotiations and business breakfasts – all forgotten in a phone call.

There is little doubt that David's company acted with extreme coldness and that this is an unusual example of misuse of the phone. It is a fact however that as a society we have learnt to use our various methods of modern communication occasionally as tools with which we can assert our authority without suffering the consequences or ignominy of a physical meeting. How often do we all communicate at a distance without really thinking of the consequences?

The need to share and to support and to receive from another has been partially replaced with an intellectual need to get information to someone else as quickly and efficiently as possible. The potential consequences of this information are not always considered. How many times have we taken part in a telephone conversation only to find out later that the person we had called had been fretting ever since due to a misunderstanding of what was said? You cannot exchange glances, give hugs, or receive physical support in an exchange which is remote and, quite often, likely to be one way.

I use the telephone. I love the telephone. And I use e-mails and faxes too. But I am aware that dependence upon them can lessen my own ability to take part in more profound sharing. I am also aware that my own physical communication skills can become weaker as a result of too great a use of these devices. Devices that, ironically, may sometimes end up producing a greater distance between me and the person I was hoping to get closer to.

We have reached a stage where we are permanently available. We view this as being important – that people can reach us whenever **they** need to. Unfortunately what **they** need is not necessarily going to be of great benefit **to us**. Often our private lives are interrupted needlessly by mobile phones carrying so-called 'urgent' messages from the office that, if truth be told, could easily have waited until the morning.

It is very hard to ignore a phone call, a fax or an e-mail. Somehow their very presence demands some form of instant attention. It is as if they have interrupted normal service and that normal service cannot be resumed until the matter is dealt with – however trivial the request may be. And yet closer inspection of the contents of many such communications may often reveal that they could be put on hold, attended to at a later date, whilst we attend to something far more rewarding for ourself, such as our life.

When you next use the phone/fax/e-mail think about how you are communicating. Be aware of the recipient's needs and feelings as well as your own. Ask yourself questions such as these: Do I really need an instant answer to this query or could it wait until the morning or until after the week-end? Do I really want to try and explain my feelings about a relationship with (......) over the phone or would I be better off meeting him/her face to face? Do I really want to communicate this piece of information through an unfeeling machine, or would it be better for all concerned if this was done in a physical, sharing way?

When you do find yourself communicating via machine, try to come away from each such communication with the feeling that you have just helped someone else to have a better day. The less you can use devices to avoid deep, meaningful, face to face communication and sharing, the more you will benefit from the improved communications you will have with everyone.

Checklist:-

1) "We have two ears and one mouth". Learn to listen more than you speak. You might find yourself receiving some very important messages.

2) Try not to judge others for having beliefs that you consider foolish or wrong. Those beliefs may be the very things that make those people happy.

3) Be open to learning something from everyone. You never know what people may have to teach you – even a child.

4) Use time away to empower you. Learn from it by using the clarity gained to effect change in your life.

5) How balanced is your use of communication equipment? Are you always available to the office? Do you want to be? Be firm with your boundaries and readdress your relationship with these devices. Try switching your phone off occasionally.

6) Always consider the feelings of the recipient of your messages. Sometimes a meeting may prove more effective.

11

Acceptance, Trust And The Release Of Guilt

"Oh yet we trust that somehow good
Will be the final goal of ill."

Alfred, Lord Tennyson

This chapter is as relevant to women as it is to men. However, the issues are of such importance, that no book aiming to help men could be complete without their inclusion.

The True Meaning Of Acceptance

Illness, redundancy, death, relationship failure, financial loss – all things that we men find particularly hard to accept. But what does acceptance really mean? Why might it be so important? Why do we often find it so difficult to accept things as they are? Why might we interpret it often as giving in, as resigning ourselves to fate?

I believe that the term acceptance is widely misinterpreted. In spite of what many of us may believe, acceptance need involve no giving in, no failure, no condoning of others' behaviour, no resignation to circumstances beyond our control. Acceptance may mean only that we understand that everything has happened up to now for a reason, even though we may not yet understand what that reason is.

We cannot change what has happened. Whatever our situation, whatever we are finding it hard to put meaning to at this time, the one thing that is certain is that everything that has happened up to now **has** happened and no amount of thinking, worrying, anger or anything else can change that fact.

We now have a choice. We can either get into a positive frame of mind about what has taken place or we can get into a negative one. The positive stance would involve accepting that events have gone this way or that way, people have behaved like this or that, and there is nothing we can do to change what has happened. This doesn't mean that we are condoning someone else's behaviour, it simply means that we are accepting that the event has transpired. We are then able to move on from that point without wasting time and energy trying to change or deny it.

The negative stance would involve us refusing to accept that what has passed was correct. That somehow it shouldn't have happened, or else someone shouldn't have behaved as they did. Essentially it involves us seeing ourselves as a victim of some sort of universal error.

I want now to come back to the idea that thought is energy. Our energy is very important and helps us to remain focused and healthy. We do not want to waste any of this energy. Let us now look at the positive and negative stances in relation to our energy and observe what we may attract into our lives as a consequence of each approach.

JOHN AND GEORGE

John and George were twins, but like so many siblings, they were very different. John was very confident, always looking on the bright side of life and generally cheerful. George on the other hand was generally down, always expected doom and gloom and found it very hard to celebrate anything joyous.

John and George had been told that they would inherit a large sum of money once their father had sold his business, which he intended to do when they reached 21 (neither wanted to continue the family business). Unfortunately, two years before they reached the required age, their father's company collapsed, leaving them with nothing.

Their reactions to this event were quite different. John, whilst disappointed, decided to get on with life, taking the 'what you've never had you never missed' point of view. George on the other hand spent months trying to discover what went wrong and soon entered a state of mild depression. He saw himself as the victim of some bad luck.

Having had the same education and done equally well in exams, they passed out into the 'real world'. John, a sports lover, soon found his way into a company that marketed sports equipment. It was a job he wanted and he aimed high to get it. His determination didn't let him down.

George on the other hand couldn't quite believe that anyone would want him; nor could he believe that there would be any decent jobs available and so, in spite of good qualifications, he ended up accepting a job way below his ability in a firm that manufactured plastic household accessories.

Three years passed. John had moved on to a sports firm that handled the marketing of sports stars; he also fell in love with an American woman who became his wife. They settled down in California where John had been offered a relocation post.

George meanwhile had remained in his plastics company, having achieved two small promotions. Still believing that the world would never provide him with anything he really liked, he also became engaged to a girl with whom he had very little in common.

Another ten years went by. John paid for a flight out to America for George (now divorced). When George arrived at John's beach-side Californian house, John's children were surfing and his wife was out playing tennis. John himself was in between visits to major golf tournaments.

George looked out at the scene in front of him, looked at John, and with a mix of anger and pathos uttered the only words that came to mind: " You lucky bastard."

Is there really luck involved? Or is it that John, the positive thinker, has accepted the information and decided to do something positive with it?

This way he is directing all his energy towards creating a better understanding and outcome in the future instead of wasting valuable energy trying to change something that has already happened.

George, the negative thinker, believes that events have gone against him and focuses a lot of his valuable energy trying to reason and think his way out of it. "If only you had done this", or "If that hadn't happened, maybe I might have....". Of course it all proves futile.

We will all recognise lines such as these because we have all used them. However if we could just catch ourselves doing it next time and stop ourselves – use a line such as "I accept this has happened, I don't understand why yet and I would like that to become clear" – maybe we would find ourselves wasting far less of our own very valuable resources.

In the example given above, John's lack of inheritance money was probably the making of him. For George, his lack of inheritance became a millstone around his neck. Same set of circumstances but two completely different reactions – one positive, one negative.

Our conditioning has been very influential in encouraging us to interpret events and reactions one way. And suggesting to a man that he may be mistaken in his interpretation of something can in itself be highly dangerous, as we men do not like to think that we have got anything wrong.

Everything happens perfectly.

Everything happens perfectly.

Everything happens perfectly.

THE CALAMINE LOTION PATH

One evening I'd assembled all of the ingredients for a glutton-

ous evening of Homer Simpson proportions: a big TV set to watch my favorite football team play in a match; my faithful dog, Astor; a feast consisting of a large double mushroom, double cheese, double anchovy pepperoni pizza; a big bottle of Coca-Cola, and a giant bag of corn chips.

It was a close game. My eyes were glued to the set as one team and then the other took the lead. Through it all, I kept shoveling pizza and chips into my mouth. It wasn't until a commercial break when I realized I hadn't left a piece for Astor, as I usually did. Suddenly I was aware of a searing pain in my stomach. Uh-oh: trouble in paradise.

The game was at a crucial point, but my stomach was on fire. I reached for the soda bottle, but it was empty. This was going to require something stronger. I ran to the bathroom, flung open the medicine cabinet, and reached for the familiar bottle of pink antacid. I sprinted back to my still-warm spot on the sofa and jumped back into the football match.

With my eyes glued to the screen, I gulped down half the container of pink liquid. The excitement of my team scoring a goal was quickly replaced by an intense feeling of nausea. I looked down at the bottle in my hand and read the label. I immediately realized I'd swallowed calamine lotion! I dropped the bottle, ran to the bathroom, and spent the rest of the evening hugging the toilet bowl.

A sleepless night followed, and the next day I visited my family physician. She shrugged her shoulders, chuckled and mustered enough empathy to prescribe some laxatives. Calamine lotion, a mixture of zinc oxide with a tad of ferric oxide, is a sticky substance that proved its staying power by sticking to my digestive tract. For the next month, all my meals tasted slightly of calamine lotion.

At the time I drank my calamine cocktail, I made my living selling welding alloys and welding machines. I never heard the phrase, "personal growth". I thought a natural therapist was some quack selling herbs and snake oil, and getting out into nature was sitting on a blanket at a football match. But the calamine calamity had gotten the best of me. I couldn't shake the taste. When my secretary mentioned that she was going on a weight-loss program that specialized in tissue and vital organ cleansing, I went along.

I accompanied Monica to Qantas House in Sydney, Australia, and listened to my first lecture on natural health. The speaker was Glynn Braddy, and he was unlike any individual I had heard before. His words made so much sense. Even though his concepts weren't easy to implement, they were simple to understand.

In no time at all I was swallowing garlic extract, giving myself coffee enemas, practicing food combining, muscle testing every thought, and pondering the karmic significance of that fateful night I could have leaned forward two more inches and grabbed the antacid mixture. I could have turned on the light and read the label. I could have left half of the pizza for the dog or the kids.

Instead I took the "calamine lotion path", which turned out to be a superhighway that presented me with the opportunity to work with authors such as Deepak Chopra, Wayne Dyer, Louise Hay, Glynn Braddy and Stuart Wilde. The calamine lotion path allowed me to start my own newspaper called "The Planet", which deals with environmental, health, and personal development issues. It has also made my gray-haired mother happy. Now every time she walks into a bookstore, she looks for her son's name on the spines of books."

Everything happens perfectly. Still don't believe it? Of course arguments can abound on this particular statement, and yet what is the point in thinking any other way? When something has happened it has happened. The important factor surely is not to believe you have been the victim of events outside your control, but to say to yourself, "What have I got to learn from this?".

For learning may be what it is all about. Could it not be that we are here to learn from these difficult events in our lives, to find a way of using them so that we progress and grow from that particular lesson and have no need to learn it again?

Believing that we are victims of events supposedly outside our control is, in the short term, much easier than accepting that we may have contributed to them. Whether it is serious illness, bankruptcy, loss of a loved one, we must remember that our feelings towards that particular circumstance are our own. It is our grief, our anger, our disappointment, our fear. And it is therefore within ourselves that we must look for answers to help us deal with these difficult moments and periods of our lives. Believing that something shouldn't have happened is perhaps easier in the short term, but where in the long term lies our hope? Is everything really outside our control? Are we always to be in danger of becoming a victim of some new twist of fate?

Men have many things in common. Some are positive, some are negative. One of the negative aspects is the desire to attribute blame. Imagine if we took that blame and turned it on its head. Imagine if we said, "Well, I didn't want that to happen, but maybe there is something I can learn from this." Wouldn't that be a healthier and more sensible approach to take, however shocking the event may have been?

I am not trying to suggest that painful things per se do not happen. They do. Many situations occur which do, at times, seem totally unfair and unjustified. But I believe there is always a reason for them. I also believe that we each possess a great deal more strength to deal with such events than we realise. In fact I have often been surprised with the way in which I have seen men rally themselves in the face of disaster. I have learnt to offer my encouragement and support but not to try to 'fix' their situation. As a result I have seen many men come through their pain with their feelings of self-worth enhanced because they have dealt with it themselves.

I do not believe that this detachment from another person's pain results in a colder or harder man. If anything I would suggest that your compassion for others may well increase as a result of realising that your responsibilities begin and end with your own feelings. Just as you cannot change what has happened to someone else, neither can you feel that person's anger, grief or disappointment. You can only feel your own. It may be worth asking yourself what that person's pain is telling you about your own life?

If something upsetting happens to you, also try to resist the temptation to try to fix it immediately. Look at what your emotions may be trying to communicate to you. You may find something beneficial in a situation that seems to have no positive side to it. It is possible that whatever happened needed to happen and you may now benefit most by making use of the information, both emotional and practical, that you have been given.

For all these events and reactions may be simply information. Information that you can choose to do something with, or that you can ignore. If you ignore it you may well find similar opportunities or bits of information presenting themselves again until you learn this particular lesson in life.

Conditioning influences how we view and respond to certain situations. It is entirely possible that there may well be much more going on in life than we have been conditioned to look for. If you can allow yourself to become a better observer, a better listener, a man who doesn't immediately jump in and try to fix everything, you may well find yourself developing a much deeper feeling for life.

Acceptance is a very hard tool to learn. As men we feel we have so much capacity to bring about change, that we can almost believe at times that we can change things that have already happened. Yet we cannot and we never will be able to. So let us make the most of the energy we do have by accepting fully and unconditionally everything that has happened to get us where we are right now, and start to use our energy, our thoughts, our emotions, in the present moment to create a better and happier future.

Trust

Once we have accepted that people have behaved as they have, or that someone has died, or that a decision went a certain way, the next question we tend to ask ourselves is why? Why did they die? Why did my football team lose? Why did I get the sack? Why is my wife having an affair?

Sometimes the answers will be clear. Sometimes they will not. Whichever is true, the need to trust is very great. Once we have accepted that a certain event has happened, we can still remain a victim of that event unless we are able to trust that it has happened for a good reason. As I mentioned above, this reason may not be clear immediately – but if we continue to work with ourselves, with our guidance, we may sometimes find that we are given answers as to why certain things have happened.

Trusting that everything happens for a good reason is another challenging concept for men. However it is possible for benefits to come out of challenging and traumatic events – benefits which we may not be able to see now but which may become clear in the future. Remember The Calamine Lotion Path?

Our biggest enemy to clarity of mind, strength and focus at this stage is our desire to judge. It is as if we all have a little judge sitting on our shoulder who is constantly trying to get us to interpret events in a certain way – and this way always seems to be a fearful, negative way. If we could only learn to drop our need to judge some things as being wrong, to drop the words 'it shouldn't have happened', it could be that more men would become open to positive change. Maybe more of us would start to observe in ourselves the development of a clearer, happier, more confident individual.

The difficulty of trusting must not be underestimated. It is as difficult to trust that something has happened for a reason as it is sometimes to accept that it has happened at all. Why trust anything that appears to be bad, or that appears to make us unhappy?

We must trust because it is possible that this was the only way that we could learn this particular lesson in life; a lesson which, if we listen, could lead us towards greater understanding and happiness and closer towards our goal of achieving our full potential.

Not to trust may be to start off down the wrong path. From there we can only continue to go further astray. As we go further down this route we may get further embroiled in arguments with ourselves or others, further into a job which we don't really enjoy, further into troubled relationships.

Our failure sometimes to accept that there could have been a good reason for events which don't please us (these events being, in my view, opportunities for us to become more whole) produces a denial which we may end up acting out in our daily lives. On the one hand we are pushing the truth away by denying its possible existence, and on the other hand we are accepting the illusion that this event either didn't happen or that it shouldn't have, both of which may be misguided.

ANOTHER PERSONAL STORY

A few years ago my wife and I were looking to move to a new area. We had found a school for the girls and were looking for a house in the area to rent. We started the rounds of viewing houses.

Eventually we found one that we loved. Admittedly it was about seven miles from the school and was right at the top of our budget, but even so we loved the setting and the rooms. We rang the agent later that day and made an offer a little under the asking price.

So certain were we that we were going to get it, we let four weeks go by without hearing a word. We wanted to trust the amount of time it was taking. In the meantime, we had started commuting daily from our present address which involved a 34 mile round trip.

Then one day the phone went; it was the agent saying we had not got the house. It turned out that two families had got involved in a bidding war and had knocked the price way out of our range.

At that particular moment it was very hard to trust that this was meant to be. We had imagined living there and now we were not to have it. We just tried to accept that there was a reason for it. It was not at all easy.

Later that week we received another phone call from someone involved in our children's school. They had heard we were looking for a house and knew of a family that would be leaving for America in a few weeks. Would we like to go and see it?

The house was weird looking on first sight. A copper roof had, as designed, turned green over the years to blend in with the countryside around it. There were very few right angles in it which added to its unusual appearance. The obvious advantages at the time were that it had perfect accommodation for us, was considerably cheaper than the other house we had been to see and was situated at the top of a footpath that led right into the school grounds. The owners seemed to like us and offered us first refusal.

We decided to take it – and now we are so glad that we did. The house is perfection. Each day we walk the short distance to school without crossing the path of a car. The community in which we live is 'international' so the girls are growing up with many different cultural influences. Being situated in a quiet cul-de-sac the children can also go out and play safely every day with their friends in the street and frequently disappear in and out of each others' houses.

This social environment has taken the pressure off us as parents and yet was not something we had considered to be important when looking at houses initially. We could so easily have missed out, without even realising that we were missing anything. We had no idea of the benefits of living close to other families until we did it.

But, by trusting that everything was happening perfectly, which was very difficult at times, we were eventually led to the perfect house in the perfect environment. All the time we felt we would get the first house, we didn't go and see any other places. This in turn meant that we were free to visit our current house as soon as it became available. We could well have panicked weeks earlier and rushed into getting a house that would not have been so suitable.

The Release Of Guilt

GRAHAM

Graham was in his late fifties. His life had been a catalogue of failed relationships, alcoholism, gambling and lost jobs. Self-destruct seemed to be his speciality.

One day, during one of our sessions, he started talking about his father. His father had committed suicide when Graham was a young man and he had been one of the unfortunate people to discover his body. Graham had been told throughout his childhood that the reason life was difficult for his parents was his fault – it was the extra burden he had placed upon them which had resulted in his father not being able to cope at times with the pressure of supporting the family (in fact he was the youngest of several children).

This message though was quite enough. And after his father's death he was haunted by a feeling of guilt for his part in what had happened. From then on he went through life feeling responsible that his father had taken his own life. He told no-one of this and so of course no-one was able to convince him otherwise.

Only when we begin to consider the possibility that circumstances may have more to them than is clear on the surface, can we begin to catch sight of the burdens of guilt that may lie underneath.

Guilt about treating people in a certain way, guilt about having done something wrong, guilt about feeling a certain way about someone or something. Guilt is just another cloak that fear uses to undermine our own feelings of self worth.

So where does this guilt come from? Is it an inevitable part of life that we just have to put up with? Or is it something over which we may have more control than we realise?

I would suggest that it is our judge at work again and that the judge is simply responding to our old conditioning, a conditioning which has been built so much around fear. As we set off in our new direction in life, as we begin to listen to ourselves and as we begin to work on ourselves, this old conditioning gets weaker and weaker, but it still has some momentum and it will still seek to reassert itself from time to time. Guilt may be one of the tools it uses to do this.

It is important to remember here that, whatever actions you have carried out, whatever words you have used, whatever reactions you have received up to now for previous deeds, it is possible that it has all happened perfectly. By looking now at your feelings, by getting in touch with things about yourself that you want to change, you can learn from the past actions and reactions and use this information to help yourself create a brighter future. Those whose lives have been affected by your actions and words also have the choice to use these experiences to learn from and to grow from, however painful this may be.

When we allow feelings of guilt to control our thoughts and actions, we are giving away our own power and responsibility. It is as if we are admitting that we have no control over our actions, that we are somehow being controlled by someone else inside of us. Guilt is a deception, and as such can only lead us further down that path of deceit and lies.

Dropping these feelings of guilt is no simple task. A thorough understanding of the choice that everyone has made at some level to be a party to our actions and words is one important consideration.

Another powerful way to remove guilt from our lives is to begin to forgive ourselves. This is something that many people find difficult to do, or feel that they are somehow powerless to do. Surely we need the person we have hurt to forgive us?

This may be misguided also. Although it is very powerful to forgive someone else, we cannot control anyone else's desire to forgive. If that person chooses to forgive us then that is good, but let us say they offer no such reassurance? What then? Do we just drown in a mire of guilt and self loathing? Or is there something we can do about it ourselves?

Go On, I Dare You. Forgive Yourself.

Here is an exercise you can do right now. Go and look in a mirror and say to yourself "I forgive myself". And repeat it; and repeat it. And if it feels stronger to do so, then list the things for which you forgive yourself. And read those items out as often as you feel you want to.

If you can't forgive yourself, anybody else's forgiveness will be that much harder to come by. Like attracts like. If there is no forgiveness inside you to start with, no-one else's forgiveness can truly come to you and do you good. It will fall on to stony ground. You have to prepare your fertile ground first and that can only come through the work that is involved in forgiving yourself.

Checklist:-

1) Acceptance does not mean resignation. It means understanding that everything that has happened, has happened. Don't try to change the unchangeable.

2) Thought is energy. Use it wisely by accepting the past instead of fighting it by saying it shouldn't have happened.

3) Stop looking to blame and start looking to the lessons you may have to learn from life. Problems are opportunities if you let them be.

4) Be aware of your judge. He may be trying to lead you astray. Allow trust a place in your life and you will undo the judge's power. Trust leads to truth.

5) Guilt is another cloak of fear. There is nothing to be gained in blaming yourself for anything you have done in the past. Forgive yourself – and others too. Start again with life.

6) Don't beat yourself up if you cannot get someone else's forgiveness. Your own forgiveness is what really counts.

12

Everything I Ever Wanted ...Except Happiness

"There has hardly been an age before ours in which so many people live in such pleasant outer conditions and yet go about with their souls barren and unoccupied."

Rudolf Steiner

We often tend to envy those who achieve material or professional success, men who seem to have it all. We spend much of our lives attempting to do the same. But what if the destination isn't what we were expecting? Perhaps we need to pay closer attention to those men who have arrived and yet still find themselves looking for something.

JACK

Jack is in his late thirties. He left school and started working straight away in the financial sector. He liked to set himself targets for his life and before long found himself achieving them.

These targets tended to revolve around money. "By 25 I want to be earning this amount a year, by 30 this amount etc." The target was set, met and he would move onto the next. In the meantime he got married and had children.

This pattern continued. He began to realise that reaching the targets was not making him feel happy. There was something missing. But, rather than question that, he carried on with this materialistic approach.

By the time he had reached his late thirties he had reached his ultimate target. He could walk into any shop and buy himself whatever he wanted.

A day spent in the High Street demoralised him. There was nothing he really wanted to buy. As life went on he found that, whilst some things gave him a good feeling for a short while, this was only ever temporary; soon after he would again find himself searching for that elusive commodity – happiness. A commodity that he could not find in any shop window.

As a result of finding that there was little he really wanted to do with his money, Jack became seriously disillusioned with

life itself. It was as if life had let him down in not providing him with the real rewards he had always thought would be his if he worked hard enough and was successful enough.

What was it Jack was searching for? Was it something he could buy? Or was it something that all the time was inside himself if only someone had told him?

The realisation that happiness may not be something that can ever be bought can be frightening for men who have spent their whole lives trying to achieve the means to buy it. Since happiness seems to be such an intangible thing, it seems much safer to avoid talking about the subject. Many men dismiss notions such as inner happiness as irrelevant, primarily because so few of us were ever told that our own happiness is important.

Furthermore, if confronted with a story such as Jack's, many men will counter this by stating that whatever was true for him, **they** would never have a problem spending large amounts of money and becoming very happy as a result. "He must be a bit of a wally". Not at all. I believe that he was just being honest about what he found to be a painful truth.

We find it very difficult to believe that what society encourages us to go out and acquire in as large amounts as possible – money – may not in the end result in our being happy, no matter how large an amount we manage to accumulate. And so blindly we battle on towards our goal of acquisition, no matter what it costs us in personal terms. And invariably it is only when we get there, if we ever consider that we have got there, that we find our destination was just a mirage.

There are men who have acquired vast sums of money and are quite clearly happy and at ease with their finances and assets. Put two millionaires side by side, an unhappy one and a happy one, and on the face of it you may see no difference in their positions. But if we could see how they had reached their destinations, we would probably find two very different routes.

I would suggest that those men who work purely to accumulate wealth whilst not really enjoying their work will probably find that their general lack of passion for their work, their general resentment that they are doing what they have to rather than what they want, will be reflected in the rewards that they achieve and the gratification that they receive from those rewards. This will also be mirrored in their general wellbeing – from their health to their love life. It is not possible to allow joylessness into a part of our lives without it affecting everything else in some way.

These men may well be powerful creators bringing in vast amounts of money, but because they have experienced unhappiness in their work and allowed that unhappiness to continue, they will invariably find a corresponding degree of unhappiness will be attached to any rewards that they earn. Like attracts like. Resent what we do to make money, exploit our way to greater riches, climb at other people's expense for the sake of acquisition and we will find that our money will bring with it similar negative experiences.

We may resent that we have finally made money but don't want to do anything with it. We may find ourselves being exploited by others. We may find ourselves being climbed over by others. We may find our body gradually caving in under the burden of guilt.

Conversely, those men who achieve their financial rewards as a result of a career that makes them totally happy, are the ones most likely to end up being totally happy with the possessions that they may have acquired through that career. Men who have taken up an occupation because they love it.

The happy ones are, I believe, those who have gone into work, knowing that they would rather be doing nothing else with their time – even if they won the lottery. They have found that their daily existence has been fulfilling and has created in them a present moment awareness of happiness. Their work is not 'work' so much as just another part of life. To these men the journey is everything.

As a result of having this fulfilment, this general feeling of contentedness, it is likely that these men find themselves focusing on their daily activities rather than on the notion of doing it solely to make money.

Remember the power of energy. Our thoughts are very powerful, and may have the ability to attract to us what we want. Those who work with a sense of happiness and reward, may find that they receive more happiness and rewards as a result. Happiness and rewards which will be reflected as much in the maintenance of a healthy body as they will be reflected in the maintenance of a healthy financial state. It is not possible to bring happiness into our lives without it affecting everything, mind, body and spirit.

So the question we need to ask ourselves about our work is – am I doing what I love, or doing what I think I must? The following story demonstrates the importance of joy in work and life:

A DREAM COME TRUE

My mother had a dream. She wanted a stage and a hall in her town for the enjoyment of drama and music. It was a reasonably sized town within commuting distance of London and consequently a prosperous area.

This dream stayed with her, on a back burner, whilst she got

on with life. She and her husband had three sons of whom I am the youngest, and a guest house of their own which they were hoping to convert into a small hotel.

Maggie and John put everything into this venture. John would even go out and work nights at a nearby builder's yard to bring in extra funds to support their lives. They set about getting planning permission and, after much effort and a few failed attempts, they finally received permission to start work. They borrowed a large sum of money to enable the works to commence.

The opening of the hotel was a grand affair and marked the culmination of much struggle and strife. Struggle that had obviously taken its toll on both John and Maggie. Not long after the hotel opened, Maggie was diagnosed with breast cancer.

My brothers and I were now teenagers. One day, just after Maggie had been admitted to hospital for major surgery, I was sitting at home waiting for news of her when a close relation walked in. He was pale faced and shaken and clearly determined to put a brave face on things. "Your mother needs all the help she can get right now. Stiff upper lip and all that – I'm sure she'll be fine. Could be a difficult night though..."I had never been so scared in my life. That night, for one of the first times in my life, I called upon God for help. I remember the guilt I had at the time, turning for help just because we were in crisis. But I prayed just the same.

To our great relief my mother did get through the night and soon started to make a good recovery. But John, my father, knew full well that if she was to have any chance of doing really well, the stresses and strains of the hotel had to go. They took the heartbreaking decision to sell up, losing most of their capital into the bargain because of their costly loans.

In the years that followed, Maggie found herself thinking more and more about her dream. Her increased appreciation of life since her diagnosis encouraged her to follow her heart as much as, if not more than, her head. Her physical health seemed to reflect this more positive and fulfilling approach to life.

She soon found herself setting up a board of directors and a charitable trust – all with the notion of building or sharing in a small hall for public performances. Council after council refused to help, but still she followed her instinct and then one day the breakthrough came. The town cinema lease was bought by the council and her board of directors was given permission to set up a small theatre within the building.

Many years later and the dream developed beyond all belief. The theatre and cinema soon came under Maggie's umbrella. As the administrator, she found herself being paid every day to do something that she loved. And then, some thirty years or so after she had first thought of the idea, she was told that the council, who years before had dismissed the notion of a theatre in the town as unnecessary, had agreed to invest nearly £3 million in renovating the whole building. This was capped a few months later by the news that she was to be made an MBE in the Queen's honours list for her services to the town.

My mother has remained in excellent health throughout what has been at times, a trying period of her life. Could it be that by following her own inner sense of joy, she has helped to create an outer world that has mirrored that joy – ie the building of the theatre and the sustaining of good health to make that possible?

Checklist:-

1) Money is no guarantee of happiness. So be clear about what you want money for when you are earning it and don't let earning it stop you from living and enjoying yourself.

2) Love what you do. If you can't love it, question whether that's what you really want to spend your life doing.

3) If you've got a dream, don't shut it away and pretend it doesn't exist. Live with it. Embrace it and share it with those closest to you. See how you get guided into pursuing it but don't be attached to having to have it exactly as you perceive it. Let the details unfold.

13

Fatherhood

"Fathering is the best thing you are ever likely to do – for your own satisfaction and joy, and for its effect on the future of other human beings."

Steve Biddulph *(Raising Boys)*

"FISHING WITH DAD"

I think the world is moving much too slowly. I concentrate on not asking one more time, "How much longer 'til we get there?" Dad has just finished saying, "Don't ask one more time!" I can tell he's still angry. He was angry this morning when we put the suitcases and things in the trunk of the black Plymouth coupe. We put a rod and tackle box back there too.

Mom now makes a little noise. She must think her words help me with Dad. They never did before, or now for that matter. I ride sitting on an apple box behind Dad, and Peter sits on another one behind Mom when he isn't sitting in her lap. Peter is three and sits in Mom's lap at the risk of being spoiled.

"You spoil that boy, Julia. You'll make him soft," Dad admonishes her. Lap sitting isn't making me soft, because I am seven. I am big and don't sit in laps. I am seven and going fishing with my Dad even though I have this idea that Dad thinks I'm kind of soft anyway.

We are on vacation to a lake in northern Michigan, and we're going to be there for a week. It is a new experience for us. It is the first vacation we've had except once when Grandfather died, and we went to Chicago and saw my aunts. Anyway, that wasn't like this was going to be. This is so exciting! Something good is going to happen to us.

"We're there," Dad says as we pull up to a small cabin close to the lake. He starts fishing right after we empty the car – fishing until dinner, and after dinner too. Peter and I look around until bedtime. Then in bed I just lie there. I can't get to sleep. Tomorrow I hope I can go with Dad. The lights are out and I still can't get to sleep.

My eyes pop open with the sounds of Dad moving around the cabin, and it seems as though he's getting ready to leave. I wonder if he will take me with him. I'm hoping if I don't ask, it's more likely he will. He goes over to where Mom lies in bed and whispers a few words. Then he shuts the door behind him.

Mom talks a little to me. She never talks too much. She says how Dad has been working hard and needs some time to himself to relax. He comes in from the lake for lunch, again for dinner, and after dark as I am getting ready for bed. This time he shows off the bluegills he caught, and talks about how good they will be fried up for breakfast. Boy, I could catch one of those!

It's morning, and as Dad is leaving, Mom gets up and speaks to him. He is instantly angry and moves over to me saying,"OK. Let's go fishing." Now? Me? I'm hurrying... my pants... my shoes. I'm ready. Oh, my coat...Oh, my hat. I'm ready; not saying anything, but very alert. I couldn't be more alert. I don't want to miss something; don't want to do anything wrong now. I'm going with him. This is going to be the best! Whatever he does, I'll do. We both have on our scarves. We both have our hats pulled a little down on one side. Everything looks right. I just can't believe it. I can't stand it! The two of us, him and me, going fishing!

The rowboat is big. The oars are big. The boat makes wooden thunking noises as we get in with our tackle. The rocking of the boat causes little waves to slap at the posts of the dock. The pole for me is leaning against a tree. It is a long bamboo pole. It sticks out over the bow pointing the way as Dad rows us out to where he knows there are fish. He looks back and forth as he positions us in exactly the right spot. He puts the anchor down a couple of times before he is satisfied.

He takes my pole and wraps a line around it lots of times so it will stay. Toward the middle of the line, he puts on a bobber shaped like a red, round ball with a long white stick coming out on either side. He carefully measures down from the bobber to a place where the weights are affixed to the line with his teeth. Then he makes sure the hook is secure; the hook that will hurt and be hard to get out if I stick it in me. He puts a worm on his hook to show me how.

I try to copy him, but worms are even tougher to handle than shoelaces. The worm looks flat where I squeeze it, and broken with its insides out where the hook came through...pretty bad-looking. I try another worm, and Dad takes the hook away to show me the right way one more time. My stomach hurts I'm so excited!

If the bobber goes down a little way, I'm not to jerk; but, if it goes down half-way on the little white stick, then "jerk!" The mist lies all along the edge of the lake, and it hangs over the water further out as well. It's cold, and I shift around on the hard board seeing the little rings on the surface where the fish push up their noses and sometimes plop out. I don't see my bobber go down at all when suddenly I hear, "You missed that bite. Pay attention if you want to fish!"

Now I'm really paying attention, and I jerk too soon. I move over to fish close by Dad. He says to take my pole over to my side of the boat. His words are harsh, and he's not looking at me. He picks up the anchor and rows to shore for breakfast.

As he and I enter the cabin, an expectant smile flashes across Mom's face and disappears just as quickly as she sees something is wrong. I am afraid to ask what I did wrong. It must have been really bad, because Dad never took me fishing again. He didn't take Peter fishing either...ever...not even once.

Many of the issues covered in this book are highlighted by this poignant story. Your heart goes out to the little boy who is left in a state of bewilderment and guilt – a state that is never alleviated by his father. It is easy to point a finger of blame at the father and criticise him for his treatment, but it is also possible to understand why he reacted like he did. Anyone who has cared for a child for any amount of time, will know how easy it is to lose patience.

The father came on the trip with all sorts of 'baggage'. He was desperate to grab time to himself and so only gave it to his son begrudgingly, after arm-twisting by his wife. Having agreed to take his son fishing, he was very attached to the idea of his son being able to fish competently – any failure to do so being perceived as a reflection of his own failure to teach his child. This attachment blinded him to the problems faced by a seven year old trying to do an adult's work.

This 'baggage' the father had probably acquired through his own childhood and adolescence. Maybe his father treated him in a similar way, and his father before him and so on down the generations. He is not conscious of this pattern nor of what impact it may now be having on his own son.

At an unconscious level, the father's agenda is this: for him to perceive the fishing trip with his son as successful, they have to do everything 'properly' and catch fish. That way he can see himself as being an effective dad. But his young son does not see it that way at all. For him to have a successful fishing trip he only has to be there with his dad. He doesn't have to prepare the rods properly. He doesn't have to catch any fish (although of course that would be great).

It is not the result that counts for the child, it is the taking part, the journey. The child would willingly repeat the same events time and time again just to have his father's support and attention. But the father doesn't value these things. He hasn't been taught to. He only values the results. And when they fail to get any results, the father loses all interest in repeating the exercise ever again. He is far too afraid of doing it all for 'nothing'.

In this instance it is the father who needed the results. And this is to me one of the most important aspects of fathering and mentoring that we, as men, need to be aware of. That is, how much are we projecting **our** needs onto our children?

We hate failing and we hate being seen as bad or unsuccessful people. And we often influence our children in ways that we hope will protect them from failure or unloving treatment. Unfortunately this often results in our trying to control their behaviour and manipulate their lives in ways that are not at all in harmony with their own development. Yes, our children came from us, but no they are not ours to control. They have their own lives to lead, their own mistakes to learn from, their own challenges to overcome. We can guide them, but we cannot change them.

There is no doubt that childhood is a time when children are learning and acquiring the tools that will shape their adult lives. If we are really concerned as to how good a job we may be doing for these children, I believe one of the most important questions we need to ask ourselves is this:- 'What example am I setting every day to the children who know me?'

In my view, it is our example that carries the greatest weight of all with children. Words, theories, books, arguments – they all have their place, but what a child sees and experiences every day is what lives with them and what they really learn from. They absorb unfailingly all of our attitudes, directly from our own unconscious into theirs.

In the story above, the child will have got the message that he screwed up in such a big way that his father could never really forgive him. In other, more subtle ways, we may be giving equally destructive messages to our children without even realising it.

How many of us are demonstrating to our children that time is something over which we have no control? That when you grow up you always have to be rushing everywhere, grabbing five minutes with your children in between everything else? Each time a child witnesses this it reinforces in them the belief that they too will struggle for time when they grow up. More importantly, perhaps, they measure their own sense of self-worth against our attitudes to them. If we have so little time available for them, what conclusions will they reach about their own value in the world?

And what about love? If you are in a relationship, are you as a man able to demonstrate to your children that you respect your partner, that you share openly and listen attentively? What messages are you giving the children in your life about the nature of adult relationships? That they are valuable and joyful parts of life that have to be worked at – or that they are problematical things which warrant little time or discussion, and which certainly feature lower down the list of priorities than work and money?

Fun is another commodity in children's lives that adults all too often forget about. Do the children around you see you as someone who takes their fun seriously and creates regular spaces for it in life? What effect will it have on them if they start to believe that being a grownup seems to imply having little or no fun?

Our children are also learning about the power of money from us. What do they observe in you? Someone who is comfortable with and open about the subject of money – however much or little you may have? Or do they see someone who is always complaining about the lack of it, suffering to earn it, or who is always keeping financial affairs to himself?

And what of work? Do your children see a father going off to work who loves what he does (without being addicted to it) and who is able to return in the evening being not only able to share what has happened to him but also being able to listen to what his children and partner have done? Or are they observing someone who trudges off to work moaning about having to go in at all? What picture are they forming of what an adult's working life entails?

However you have been in the past with any of these examples, or any other aspect of life that children may observe, remember the power to effect change lies in the present moment. It may be worth thinking about examples you have set in the past – but don't wallow in guilt about it – think about the example you can start setting now. It doesn't matter if your children have long since flown the nest. You can still change, and they – and others – can still learn from you.

If I could get just one point across to men about fathering/mentoring children it would be this. It is who you are as a man, your daily example, that affects children more than anything else you can ever teach them. It is not who you are for the two weeks holiday once every fifty two weeks that makes the difference.

If you want to help raise happy, balanced children, seek to become a happier, more balanced man. All the books, all the theories – and even all your material success – they mean nothing to children. What means everything to them is who you are, how you are and what you can do with them.

MY FATHER'S HAND

I remember looking at the back of my hand a few months ago and I was surprised that I didn't know it anymore. This sun-browned hand with all the darker spots on it wasn't the hand I

remembered. It looked more like my father's hand … and yet not. My fingers are longer than his were and the veins on my hand more prominent. But my hand looked as old as I remembered his to be.

I know that I'm getting older, of course; my 60th has come, been celebrated and is now another memory. The birthday itself seemed meaningless at the time, but biology will not be denied. The lines in my face deepen, my hair continues to thin, and I don't recover from eating big as quickly as I used to. I don't wake up with an erection every morning. I play computer games more often and want to work less, and in this regard I am much more aware of how tired I am of working for a living. It's been 44 years now and I've been responsible for supporting a family most of that time. My eyesight is beyond drugstore correction, and I've got to wear a partial denture on one side.

Ah, I know, I'm rambling. I know what it's really about, this dull, gray mood that hangs over me like a long, cold, slushy Chicago winter. I miss my dad. He died this past September on the morning of that blue-collar holiday, Labor Day.

At his memorial service, I heard people say of him that he was a simple man, and I felt insulted and embarrassed because I thought of "simple" as a diminishment of him. It was only later, after my sorrow had abated some, that I heard the tone in their voices and now I know how they meant it. They meant it the same loving way Studs Terkel means it when he talks of the little people of this land. Little-known, but never little in spirit.

Studs would have loved my father, because he was the kind of down-to-earth guy who built cities like Chicago. Studs wouldn't have called him "Mr". After a few minutes he would have called him "Tony" just as all his friends did, because my father drew people to him. As soon as you started talking to him, you began to feel he'd be easy to be around.

My father wasn't a philosopher; he'd be more likely to build the bookshelves to hold the philosopher's books. And it wouldn't be an ornate bookshelf, it would be like him: sturdy, dependable and strong. It would hold up under stress and not fall over.

His tools were a sense of humor, a kind heart, a hammer, a saw, a ratchet wrench, a guitar, and drums. With these, and a sometimes stubborn determination to know just what he had to know, he fashioned a living for his family through the Depression, WWII, and beyond, as a guy who fixed his own car (and mine), built end tables, peeled layers of wallpaper for my mother, built a house for his family, fixed plumbing for his sister, and was a working musician – the guy who played in the lounge where you waited for your name to be called for dinner. And because you liked his fine tenor voice, maybe you hired him to play at your daughter's wedding reception. And maybe at your New Year's Eve party.

He drove a bread truck when the music business was slow, and delivered bridgework for a dental lab when rock bands and disc jockeys took over the lounges.

He finally retired when he found himself chasing a guy who had cut him off in traffic and given him the finger. "When I let some jerk like that get to me, I knew it was time to quit," he said at the time.

He never spoke of love to me; those words only escaped his lips in song, or once in a spontaneous moment on the phone with me. We were both shocked and hurried on to other subjects. Like most of the men of his generation and the generations before him, his expressions of affection were in his "doing," and his love came from his handiwork. There are signs of it everywhere in my mother's home and in my own. If you needed it, you just mentioned it to my father and it would appear from his workshop in the next week or so.

I taught him to hug in the '60s and he became a hugging legend in our family. We came from miles around to get his hugs, especially the children. He had a way with children that I hope to cultivate in myself. Not that he doted on them or continually bounced them on his knee, he didn't. But they trusted him, they sensed that he was kind.

I miss his laughter. He would tell some of the same stories over and over again and would get so wrapped up in them, as would everyone else, that he would have tears in his eyes and be gasping for air from laughing so hard.

I have little left in the way of tangible memories of things shared. In 60 years he wrote me three notes, two of which I still have. One thanked me for a dub of "Lonesome Dove". The other was a birthday card for my 60th. "I never thought I'd get old enough to have a 60-year-old son," he said.

He just made it.

We did actually spend some time alone once. We took a trip in my '64 VW bug from Chicago to Moab, Utah, in about 1981. My mother set it up. She threw his bag in the back of the car and pushed him out the door. We traveled for four or five days and said maybe 150 words to each other, mostly about gas mileage and the weather. On the first night we camped somewhere outside of Des Moines, Iowa, in a campground. It was the first time he had been camping in about 40 years. After we got the tent set up, I noticed a cloud whiz by and then heard a siren go off in the town nearby. I thought it was just a test and ignored it. That night, the wind drove the rain horizontal and a tornado passed nearby. From then on, any wisp of a cloud anywhere in the sky and my father was set for a motel!

But on the last night of the trip, we camped at the edge of the Snake River canyon and watched a typically beautiful Western sunset after dinner, sitting side by side on our campstools. Suddenly, I felt an arm go around my shoulders. I thought someone had snuck into the camp! Then I heard him say, "I'm sorry".

Surprised, I stammered, "What do you mean?"

"Well, I wasn't there when you were growing up and..."

I stopped him. I didn't want him to go through any more pain about it. I knew he had been thinking about it for a long time.

"It's OK, dad. I understand."

And I did. And in that moment all was healed between us. I could hear his heart and I knew how he loved me after that day.

Checklist:-

1) Try to see the world through a child's eyes. Children aren't always after results, they are often just hungry for time and attention. Drop your personal needs to meet goals and value the time you have to give as much as the 'success' of any activity you may be involved in with a child.

2) Check what you may be projecting onto the children in your life. Are you doing things with them that meet their needs, or yours?

3) Children have their own lives to lead. Let them live them – don't be tempted into trying to make everything alright for them.

4) What example of adulthood are you setting children by the way in which you live? Would you be looking forward to growing up if you were a child observing your life?

5) Watch in particular what messages you are regularly giving your children about important subjects such as time, relationships, money, fun and work. Remember, it is who you are on a **daily** basis that really counts, not who you are for two weeks out of fifty two.

14

Men And Death

"...men fear death as children fear to go in the dark."

Francis Bacon

THE DEATH OF MIKE

I saw a friend die today.

I've seen dead people and dead animals before. And I've seen animals die. But today was the first time I saw a person die before my eyes. And he's a friend of mine.

Today was the last day of an intense week of training at work. My group was to give our final presentation in the Board Room at 2:00. Returning from lunch just after noon I noticed some commotion in the elevator lobby. As I approached I could see a man down with three people over him. He was obviously in distress.

It was Mike. I heard him say some words. "I'm diabetic."

Mike vomited. He evacuated. His entire system was saying, "I don't want this thing – this death – to come into me!". He choked and retched and blew a wad of something from his stomach almost up to the ceiling. They rolled him on his side to keep his air passage open.

Three people were with Mike. Tom, from Building Services, and two representatives in the building that day bringing us information about a United Way agency – CAPRI – a research organization for heart disease and healing. Mike couldn't have been in two better pairs of hands.

The fire department was there in two minutes. The medics weren't far behind. There were others who gathered. Gapes. Gawks. I was one of them. Just watching. I began to feel useless, helpless. Another manager from my department showed up. We started talking about contacting Mike's wife.

A paramedic wanted information. Someone started calling out for anyone from Mike's department who could help with information. I walked past the security person who had begun shooing elevator people to another floor. We squatted by a medical case. What's his name? Michael. Gengo. G E N G O. George. His first name is George. He goes by Mike.

The paramedic patiently wrote what I couldn't clearly say. I realized Mike was only two or three feet from us. Could Mike hear me? In another setting the conversation would have been pathetic. I would have sounded drunk. But I decided Mike probably couldn't hear me. I thought in that narrow moment that death must be lonely. Maybe desolate is a better word.

Mike was in caring, professional hands. Yet, how could he know? He had been unconscious now for 10 minutes or more. Time. Such an odd thing. I finally decided there was nothing more I could offer Mike or those helping him. I returned to my meeting.

I had an hour to sit through before my presentation. Before it started the leader of the meeting asked me if I was all right. He knew of Mike's situation. I said, "No. I'm not all right". He asked me if I thought I needed to be somewhere else. I told him no, I would stay with my group to do the presentation. I would survive. I say that a lot. This time my "I'll survive" was more than trite.

So I sat. I prayed that I would hear the siren of the Medic One van leave before I had to give my presentation. I thought the most awful thing to happen would be for me to hear the siren as I started my talk. Thankfully it came well before that.

Mike! What's happening to you? How are you? What will be your... future?

All but one presentation group had experienced technical difficulties. We were no different. But we got through it. We received congratulations and kudos for having survived the nightmare. I smiled. Said, "thanks!" Firmly shook hands. And was fully thinking about Mike again. The meeting broke for refreshments.

I walked out and saw Deetsy talking with one person off to the side. I knew that Deetsy had been on the mezzanine and knew about Mike's distress. So I went straight to her. More congratulations. I let a couple of sentences exchange in dialog. Then I asked her if there was any word on Mike. Her face told me faster than any words could ever tell me. She told me very simply, "Mike didn't make it". She told me how they wanted to keep it from the group until after all the presentations. There was one more group to go.

Then an odd thing happened. Deetsy apologized to me that she had to tell me this bad news. Anyone listening in would not have interpreted it as odd. But I did. Why should a friend apologize to me for telling me of another friend's death? I immediately and earnestly told Deetsy, "Please don't apologize. Thank you for telling me. I wanted – no needed – to know".

The conference leader made it clear that I could leave if I wanted to. I decided to leave. Deetsy told me there were some colleagues gathering in our programming department. One in particular I wanted to see was Jeff. Jeff was Mike's very good friend. Jeff was also my former boss. I wanted to see them all. I wanted to be a part of their shock and grief.

I quickly said good-bye to a few as they tailed back into the Board Room. Another seminar leader brought up the rear. As soon as she noticed I intended to leave she asked me to stay. She said there would be some important follow up at the end. I didn't argue. I crept in the back door and sat on the cold air conditioning vents.

But soon I felt that I needed my own grief space. So I went back to the lounge. Thankfully I was alone – for a while. A senior manager saw me and walked in. He said that Deetsy told him I knew Mike was dead. He sat and talked with me for a couple of minutes. He reminisced of when he first met Mike – a long time ago when Mike was Admin. Manager in Canada. Then he left to return to the presentation in progress. I sat for a while more watching the water and the mountains. Thinking. Always not quite crying. And frequently reliving watching Mike die.

I thought of loneliness. Desolation. I've thought a lot. This typing has helped. I have not yet outwardly cried for Mike. That will come. I know it will. That may be tonight when I go back

to bed. It may come sometime later – maybe at some embarrassingly inappropriate time. But I know that sometime... I will cry for Mike.

The above story is an example of how death can occur at the most unexpected of times. Mike's friend shows great honesty and a real desire to be a part of the process of death. His story also demonstrates the surreal nature of death as it mingles with life – in this example it is witnessed occurring in the midst of a typical day at the office.

In general our society does not have a great appreciation of death. To many men it is a major worry that potentially represents the ultimate failure. It is the absolute proof that, in spite of all our efforts to control and manipulate circumstances and the world around us, when it comes to relinquishing our bodies we seem to have very little say in the matter. Something bigger seems to take over. Something that most of us are so scared about that we will avoid personal involvement at all costs and often won't even discuss it. If we hear the subject of death being discussed, or related subjects such as hospitals or illness, we will often try to busy ourselves with other matters and avoid involvement in such conversations.

Death is another example of how we tend to fight an event that has already taken place. The loss of a loved one is very difficult to bear at the best of times, but it is not helped by our internal resistance to accepting that person's death. Tiredness is one of the most common consequences of grief and I believe a part of this tiredness may be brought on by our inability to accept the passing of someone we have cared for. Whilst there is no easy or simple solution to coming to terms with anyone's death, I believe that if we could get ourselves into a state of acceptance that it has happened, we would find ourselves much better equipped to cope.

The attitude of men to potentially life-threatening illnesses in others is worth looking at to see if there are changes that we could make that would make better use of our abilities.

Take cancer for example. Having listened to and read various reports from cancer patients, it seems that many of us fall into one of three categories on hearing that someone has this much feared illness.

The first category consists of those who just can't mention it in conversations, who carry on with small talk but shy away from any mention of the big C. The second category consists of those who seem to have an almost morbid obsession with bad news and use the opportunity to off-load the terrible things that are happening to them, too. The third, much smaller group, consists of those people who are the most valuable to someone finding themselves in the grip of serious illness; a group of people who just listen when asked to listen, help when asked to help and who back off when asked to give space. They are unconditional in their approach to the patient.

There is no doubt that life-threatening illnesses are frightening for all concerned. As men we have learnt to fix things and we want to 'fix' death. So whilst modern medicine and complementary and alternative therapists continue to search for life's magic elixir that will help 'fix' death, every day other men are finding out at first hand that death has become a part of their new experience. A new experience about which so little seems to be understood.

The need to control every aspect of our lives has led us into fascinating times with amazing inventions but no one has yet invented anything, it seems, which helps us better understand death. The one thing that is certain about life, the one thing that every race and creed has in common, is that at some point we are going to die. And yet how much money does society put into exploring this universally important aspect of life – the process of dying? So little is still understood about it.

To see why this is the case, it is worth reminding ourselves of our collective habit of avoiding facing our fears. Our fear of letting go of people and objects, our fear of looking into areas of life that we do not understand, our fear of finding out information which may not fit into our view of the world, our fear of what may happen to us after we die – maybe most of all our fear that when it comes down to it, we are not going to be able to control death.

All these fears, and probably many others, have led men into extraordinary ways of preserving life – sometimes at great cost – as opposed to leading us into ways of gaining a greater understanding of the process of what we know as death. Our ignorance in this case has created a vast collective fear.

If I were to say that death, for all its finality on a physical level, can be a beautiful thing, many would probably consider me at worst mad and at best unrealistic. And yet to those many people who have witnessed and experienced the process of dying, it is clear that a deeper understanding of our involvement in the dying process can lead to a very peaceful and acceptable transition.

FAREWELL

Tim will not forget the last day that he spent with his wife. He had been wondering what it would feel like ever since she was diagnosed with cancer a few years previously. True, the first couple of years of her illness had been okay, but this last few months had been hell for all concerned, including his two young children.

But in her last week something had happened. Helen, his wife, had changed; she seemed more peaceful now, even accepting of what was happening. The fight that had been waged for so long, so painfully at times, had given way to a state of grace. It was possible that this state had been reached earlier in the week when Helen had appeared to come to terms with the fact that she was not a failure for leaving them like this. This fear of failing – ie not living – had dogged her ever since the illness began, but now she seemed able to let go. By so doing, Tim learnt to let go too.

And so it was that day. Tim observed in a state of awe as Helen breathed out – never to breathe in again. And so that was it – death. There she was in front of him – and yet she wasn't there at all.

When describing this experience to a friend the next day, the sadness and sense of loss apart, Tim had one word that summed up his general feeling that day: elation.

Tim's story demonstrates that death does not need to be experienced as some sort of failure. Death is another part of life. And if we choose, we can either make it another good part of life, or a bad part. Sometimes we may not be able to control how death occurs (cancer, car crash, old age) – but we will quite often be able to play a very important part in the surroundings and atmosphere in which either we or someone close to us is allowed to die.

By playing our part in this process it is very possible that we can help to make someone's passing free of some of the pain. This we can do by listening closely to their needs. There is no doubt in my mind that helping someone to 'move on' in a caring and peaceful way is one of the greatest gifts, if not the greatest gift, that we can ever give anybody. In no circumstances can such an experience be deemed a failure.

It seems obvious really, doesn't it? And yet even today, after all the wonderful work and research that many people have carried out on the subject of terminally ill people, we may still find some specialists distancing themselves from their patients who are nearing death. For those patients represent to them their greatest fear – that their mission, to preserve life, sometimes fails. They will never be able to preserve life successfully forever. We will all die. And, because of their inability either to recognise or confront this fear, they will continue to distance themselves from their dying patients at a time when patients and their families most need their support.

MELANIE

I had been regularly visiting Melanie, a woman suffering from

cancer. She had been hospitalised at a well-known cancer hospital for several months.

One day her consultant failed to turn up with the team of young doctors for Melanie's regular consultation. At first she thought little of this, but when it continued for three days, she made further enquiries.

A nurse eventually came into her room to say that, regretfully, her treatment had been halted. The fact was that tests showed that she was not improving and the hospital decided they could no longer carry on filling her full of drugs. She felt let down and abandoned. Hardly the ideal emotions for someone desperate for help, hope and support. Fortunately, prior to her death, she was able to relocate to a hospice where she received more compassionate care right up to her death.

The consultant was male. His team generally consisted of men too. I am sure there are female consultants who would react in a similar fashion if they have not dealt with their own fear of death, but this is a heavily male-dominated profession.

So why did the consultant respond in such a callous way? Is it possible that his patient represented his own feeling of failure and that further contact with her as she died would only have reinforced this belief?

As long as we as a society fail to recognise our fears, some doctors will continue to ignore patients' and their own needs in similar ways. Of course not all doctors fall into this category and improvements in our general appreciation of the process of dying can only improve things further.

One of the most significant ways to begin to overcome our fears related to death is to change our view that death somehow represents some sort of failure. That death is wrong. It shouldn't happen.

It is worth noting that acceptance of death may be more easily reached if we also have a good sense of what we believe goes on after death.

Some men change their views of what happens to us when we die as a result of studying reports of those who have had near-death experiences. Others through their own spiritual beliefs. These men tend to feel great relief as a result of this change in understanding. They are often able to accept the deaths of loved ones or their own impending death with far greater calm. Another common change is that they often start to live their own lives differently on the basis of what is to come.

But we can also begin to find ways in which we can help to make the process of dying a more acceptable and natural process of life. People in their last few days sometimes have the most incredible wisdom and insights to pass on. It is such a shame to miss those words just because we are too scared to listen.

Trying to manipulate circumstances, seek countless 'expert' opinions, find out why an operation didn't work or why the wrong meal was served up – all these things have their place but they also take up a huge amount of energy. Energy the patient might far rather was spent on listening to them, or just being with them.

Again, when under the shadow of death, it is worth noting how men will try to find a way of sorting it out. We feel that by complaining to someone, shouting at someone, we might somehow change the result. And yet our anger is invariably anger with ourselves, fuelled by our fear of what is going on around us. We don't like what we are experiencing and we do not want to accept it as being right.

We need to learn to **listen**. And we need to learn to accept what someone else may be asking for. By not doing so we are being no better than Melanie's doctor who failed to meet his patient's needs when she most needed him. If we could only stop making so much effort to manipulate circumstances to fit our own needs, we might find that we are far better equipped to deal with the whole subject of death than we had ever imagined.

In the business world men are used to making decisions to

change things. But life does not conform to a corporate model. Neither does death. And we cannot decide when or where or how it may come. No amount of fighting it is going to make one bit of difference. But by playing our part, watching and listening for our cues, we can help to make it a process that is as positive as birth.

Checklist:-

1) Death is not a failure. It is the manner in which someone arrives at death which is important.

2) Don't steer clear of conversations about death. If you have nothing to say, say nothing. But listen – and learn.

3) If someone close to you is dying, listen to them even more closely than normal.

4) Question yourself on your views of what happens on and after death. Read books on near death experiences and life after death, talk to family and friends. Remember that fear is ignorance – so undo the ignorance with as much information as you feel you need.

5) Allow death to become a natural and open part of life. Don't be afraid to study it, discuss it and learn about it.

16

Working Together

"The woman's cause is man's: they rise or sink together."

Alfred, Lord Tennyson

There is no doubt that seeking out other men, both older and younger, and sharing experiences and opinions is a vital part of male development and one which is often lacking in our modern society. In addition to the feedback I obtain from the men amongst my family and friends, I also belonged to a men's group for a couple of years. Much of the experience I have gained in that environment has helped me to become a better listener and has helped me to reach a far deeper understanding of myself.

There is also, I believe, a great need for us to learn to share more openly with women. After all, what chance is there for women to understand us better, if we are not willing to sit down and discuss our needs, problems and challenges with them? How can we expect the opposite sex to help us to meet our needs, if we are not willing to open up to them about what we find difficult in life? Is it again our fear of appearing vulnerable to a woman that stops us from such openness?

I believe that women have a great deal to teach us. And we have a great deal to teach women. Just as much. Men need women, we love women, and we want to know how better to get on with them. We could become much wiser men, better fathers and far greater lovers by understanding more about the joys, pains and tribulations of female experiences such as pregnancy, sexual desire, motherhood and ambition. This improved understanding can only come about through more sharing and listening.

The world is changing; some men **are** becoming more willing to look at themselves and their lives and to question what it is they are struggling for. This desire to look is fuelled by the feeling that life is somehow incomplete in a way that goes deeper than purely material solutions. I believe that we can get closer to a complete understanding of happiness and joy by gaining a far greater understanding of the things that would make the women in our lives happier.

Whether our sister, friend, mother, daughter, partner – we men are largely unaware that we have so much more to offer them besides material possessions and masculine sexuality. It may only be through understanding the female sex better as a whole, which can happen not only at home but also at a community level through mixed support groups, that we will find ourselves able to offer those women what they want. By doing so, we may find ourselves feeling more complete, more satisfied and more able to cope with the challenges that the world throws up every day. We may become better men.

We need the support of women. We need their help, and we always will. For man's survival, men need women. Isn't it about time we started to engage that help fully?

It is possible that the time has come for a much deeper level of communication to take place between men and women so that we can further improve the society in which we live. This can only be done by having a thorough understanding of the problems that each sex faces in society today.

Let men and women meet on equal terms; let men and women discuss issues that relate to their respective positions in the community today; let men and women explore each other's worlds through sharing experiences with each other. Let men and women respect each other. And let our children witness this new level of co-operation.

It is only through acquiring a thorough understanding of each other that we can become whole. And it is this 'wholeness' that I believe is the single most important aim of our lives. If by striving to gain greater understanding of our sons, fathers, daughters, mothers, sisters, grandparents we become more whole as individuals, surely this has to lead to better lives for each and every one of us and for our children and future generations? To encourage a more thorough understanding of what makes a man a happy man, what makes a woman a happy woman, what makes a family a happy family – surely this can only lead to a more balanced and healthy society?

Maybe a society where men will give each other time off willingly when a crisis arises at home; a society where a man will be congratulated for helping to create and maintain a happy household; a society where men witness improved company performances as a result of placing more emphasis on meeting the needs of the **teams** (families, partners) that, either directly or indirectly, make up the work force; a society where we could feel joyful at the prospect of our children taking their own places in it in years to come; a society where a man can openly celebrate being a father, a lover, a worker, a provider and a friend; a society where a man can openly celebrate his feelings.

It may seem a long way off, yet change can start right here. If we, the men of this generation, are not willing to make ourselves heard, then the society we would like our children to grow up into will not be there. Society cannot become better unless people take the initiative to improve it. The question is, do any of us feel strongly enough to make an individual effort that may result in a more widespread change?

Checklist:-

1) Look for opportunities to share life experiences and stories with other men.

2) Look for opportunities to do the same with women.

3) Remind yourself of the importance of the role of the women in your life. Tell them how much you value their contribution.

4) If you are in a position to do so within your company, encourage the nurturing of a relationship with your employees' families. The more you are able to support them, the more support you are likely to receive from them in the future. Treat the families that help to make up your work-force with care and respect.

Imagine A World Where...

Men and men listen to each other;

Men and women listen to each other;

Children witness parents who laugh together, cry together,

work together and talk together;

Businesses rate the well-being of the employees and their

families as highly as their profits;

We respect each other for our differences

as well as our similarities;

We give – without feeling we have to receive in return;

We receive – without feeling we have to give back;

We see everyone we meet as someone

who can teach us something;

Our physical appearance is always a blessing;

The present moment is treated for what it is – a gift;

Death is accepted as a positive part of life.

Imagine a world where we all know that we are choosing our

lives and we all celebrate being who we are...

I wonder where this world could be?

Tool Kit

Meditation

Start by taking off your shoes, loosening tight clothing and sitting comfortably. A relaxed position with as straight a spine as possible is ideal. Hands can be rested gently, one in the other on the lap, while limbs and feet should be positioned so as not to be uncomfortable. If preferred, you can lie down provided your spine is kept straight.

It is always best to start by taking a few deep breaths. This helps to calm the active mind. When taking these breaths, be aware of the idea that old energy (stress, pain, fear) leaves while you are breathing out, while new energy is gained as you breathe in.

This exercise begins with a relaxation technique called the bodyscan. It is an excellent way to rid the body of stored tension and leads into the early stages of the meditative state. It is particularly recommended for beginners who find the whole self-discipline aspect of meditation difficult .

Once your eyes feel comfortable to remain closed, place the focus of your attention on the thumb of the right hand. Imagine all tension leaving the thumb and, after a few seconds, move on to the first finger and repeat the process along each finger, across the palm of the hand, the back of the hand, the wrist, forearm, elbow, travelling up the right arm to the shoulder.

After the shoulder, focus on the right upper back, followed by the middle back and lower back.

At this point take a couple more deep breaths, again being aware of gaining strength on the in-breath and letting go of stress with the out-breath, and then repeat the technique on the left side of the body, starting with the left thumb and finishing with the left lower back. Take a couple more deep breaths.

Focus now on the stomach and follow this with the chest, neck, throat and jaw – a place where we all tend to hold a great deal of tension. Now focus on the mouth, cheeks, nose, ears, eyes, scalp and head. Take a couple more deep breaths.

Next, focus on the sitting muscles, the right upper leg, the knee, calf, ankle, foot and toes. Start again with the left upper leg and repeat the process.

Please take time on this technique. As you become more practised, you may find that you become aware of isolated pockets of stress in your body. You may start to 'see' the body part in front of you or you may feel a tingling sensation as you identify specific areas. If you do feel any pain or blockage in a specific place, acknowledge it and accept it prior to moving on to the next part of the body. This ability to identify, which will increase each time you practise, gives you greater control and power in dealing with imbalances.

With the bodyscan complete you are now ready to provide something else to focus on. You need this focus because your 'left-brain' is so used to being active that it will immediately start to focus elsewhere (work, relationships, bills, shopping). You need to beguile it into just being. This is made easier by the use of simple techniques.

You can choose to focus on your breathing which just involves counting silently the in-breath and the out-breath – starting again each time you get side-tracked by thoughts. Don't try to fight the thoughts, don't try to change them. When you feel ready (or more likely when you remember where you are!) just start observing and counting the breath again.

Alternatively you can use a word or phrase ('mantra') which you repeat silently throughout the remaining time. Words such as 'trust' or 'accept' or a phrase such as 'I let go' or 'let go' are good examples to start with. The choice of words is limitless and can either be a made-up word or one that holds significant meaning for you in the moment.

In a busy mind, thoughts can seem to be interrupting end-lessly, but disciplined use of the mantra or breath will eventually produce a more relaxed sensation and will lead to a deeper state of being.

This should be continued for the remainder of the twenty minutes (have a clock or watch nearby). At the end take one or two minutes to readjust before opening your eyes or trying to move. A state of deep rest has been entered and time needs to be taken to return from it.

Please Note The Following:

The most important factor in successful meditation is taking the time to practise it properly. Two sessions each day for between fifteen and twenty minutes each are ideal although unlikely to happen to start with. The benefits are cumulative and are unlikely to be realised fully by anything less.

If you don't feel you want to bother doing that, or if you become bored with the practice itself, it is likely that you have not studied enough evidence on the benefits of meditation. I used to think it was strictly for 'weirdos', but now I've been practising it for some years I would no sooner miss a meditation than I would a meal. Get out some books on the subject, look at the evidence, then start giving it a chance to work on your life.

It is advisable to take the phone off the hook when meditating. Interruptions are sometimes unavoidable but it helps to take all the preventative action that you can.

Don't worry about falling asleep – particularly in the early days. This may be your inner guidance telling you that sleep is important to you at this time, probably as a result of having been doing too much.

Expect nothing – meditations are often different and never predictable.

There is no such thing as a 'bad' meditation – every meditation does you good although you may not think so at the time.

You may need to give this technique a few weeks to start working easily – do not despair if the first few days seem to be difficult. Allowing the active mind to become used to a more restful state can be like turning a tanker. It takes time.

Be patient, be disciplined!

Balancing The Intellect And The Intuition

Most of us tend to view life as a half empty glass as opposed to a half full glass. Instead of actively enjoying the present moment and all that it entails, we very often find ourselves worrying about events in the future that may not even happen. Asking men to stop thinking about the future, or even the past, is all very well but why should it have any physical repercussions and how on earth do we put it into practise?

To begin to reach an answer to these questions, it is necessary to consider again how our minds and bodies may function. It is commonly accepted that the brain is divided into two halves – the left and right sides. These sides have quite different functions – the left side of the brain being the rational, thinking, doing part, while the right side is the intuitive, feeling, sensing part.

Our intellect, the left side, will be absorbing information all day and helping to make rational decisions based on the information that has been presented to it: which shop to go to, which clothes to buy in that shop, whether to pay by cash or credit. All these decisions are made by our intellectual self, based on the information that has been presented.

Our intuitive self may also help us to make decisions every day, but these decisions will be based more upon a feeling. Examples such as what colour clothes we feel best in on a certain day, what type of lunch we feel like eating, whether or not we feel like going to the cinema in the evening. Any decision that is based upon a feeling comes mainly from the right side of the brain – although of course there may often be intellectual considerations in that decision.

If we could learn to provide the left side or intellect with all the information it requires, whilst also allowing our intuition, our feelings, to speak through – then the balance we would be effecting would enable us to see the truth of who we are more clearly. That improved balance is bound to lead to a happier and more satisfying life.

It is often the case that if you make a decision based solely upon intellectual considerations whilst ignoring a strong 'gut' feeling that would guide you otherwise, you will invariably encounter obstacles in your way and will often end up with an unsatisfactory result. This may be because the needs of your emotional self have not been met.

It can also be that if you follow a purely gut reaction whilst ignoring important intellectual considerations which you know must have a bearing on your actions, you will sometimes find it difficult to accept fully the action that you have taken and the result that you have achieved. This may be because the needs of the intellect have not been fully met.

Exercise

Turning Our Fears Into Something Good

The first question to ask is how to stop putting out messages of fear?

To begin with you need to have great clarity about your fears. Know your enemy well, for your greatest enemy could be your greatest friend. List your fears. Take a long time doing this for it is very important and will help you make a blueprint from which you may ultimately start shaping a better life. Start with the most obvious fears and then gradually begin to add to that list. Write down everything and be aware of any feelings that come up for you as you write them down. Very often, this alone will allow you to see that your fears are not nearly as frightening as you first imagined them to be.

You now have in front of you life as a half empty glass. Your list of fears holds clues as to how you presently approach many things in life in a negative, fearful way. For example: a fear of lack of money could result in you saying "I ought not to buy that, I might need the money for something else"; a fear of being a bad person might result in "Even though I'm tired and need to rest, I should go to dinner with them because they might think I don't like them". These fears could well result in the exact experience you are trying to avoid being brought closer to you .

The aim here is to help you to list your fears, and then help you to turn them into the half full glass as opposed to the half empty one. This you do very simply. The next stage therefore is to take your first fear and turn it into something that you want. Examples:-

Fear

I fear not having enough money.

I fear suffering with my illness.

Want

I want enough money to... (list each thing that you want money for).
I want better health so that I can... (list what you would do with better health).

After a few days, when you have a detailed list of fears (you can of course add to them at any time in the future as things come up) and have turned them into wants, you can throw away your list of fears. The objective of this exercise being to recognise the fears, turn them into positive wants – and then focus on the wants in as detailed and emotional a way as possible. Once you have a clearer idea of what you want, then you will be able to bring yourself more into the present moment through the use of affirmations (see end of exercise).

Once you start thinking about the things that you really want in a detailed and exciting way, you may be starting to create that reality. The more details you give yourself, the more chance you have of realising those details in physical terms.

It is very important to bear in mind the following when doing your list of wants:

1) You have NO control over anybody else's reality, therefore it is

no good trying to create something for somebody else. Examples of this may be:

I want my partner to stop worrying about me.

I want my father to be less angry.

I want my child/parent/partner to be out of pain.

You have no control over any of the above. You have control only over how you are feeling about the above. More achievable wants would therefore be something like:

I want to accept my partner's concerns.

I want to be at peace with my father's anger.

I want to have compassion for my child's/parent's/ lover's suffering.

In none of the above do you have any control over the actual reality that each of those is experiencing – but you do have complete control over how you feel about their relative conditions. The magic lies in identifying that control – knowing where your responsibilities begin and end – and then using all your energy towards a positive and acceptable result.

This does not mean you suddenly become hard and callous, with not a care for anybody. It means you become so focused that you know exactly what you can and cannot physically do for others, that you know the boundaries between someone else's pain and your appreciation of it, and that you do not get yourself into stressful conditions about something over which you have no control.

2) You cannot create negatively. This may seem obvious, but it is interesting how many people start their wants lists with "I don't want." Examples of this may be:

I don't want to have cancer any more.

I don't want to get any fatter.

I don't want to lose my money.

All of these involve creating negatively. This cannot be done. Achievable wants would therefore be something like:

I want to have better health.

I want to be happy with my body.

I want to have enough money to... (list what you want the money for)

This is positive creating, not negative. Each of the above is therefore achievable, however unlikely it may seem at the moment, because we are all powerful creators. It is only when you try to create negatively that you find your wants seem unattainable. So please, remember, no negative creating.

Once you have created your wants list, continue to add to it, change it, give it more detail, until you have a list that gives you a feeling of joy and anticipation.

With this list completed, you may start to have greater clarity. Work with this list regularly. Refer to it as often as possible so that it becomes an integral part of your daily awareness. Regular practise is very important. You will soon begin to realise how previously you went through life with a vague idea of what you wanted but with no real knowledge. You may soon develop a far greater understanding of what you are really like.

Try to **feel** what it is that you are wanting before you try to **do** anything towards getting it. Through the exercise given, some things will start to give you a good feeling. Recognise and be aware of this feeling before you do anything with it. This way you will know what is worth pursuing. It is not necessary to do any-thing physically towards making this list come true other than getting to know it so well that you know every detail on it.

Opportunities may come along and you will know to take them. Things may start to happen that will make you realise that you are now beginning to work closer to your fullest potential. And when you start to feel a little more confident, try taking your want and bringing it into the present moment through the use of affirmations. An affirmation is a statement of where you have now come to. Examples:

I like the person I am becoming.

I have better health.

I am happy with my body.

I am at peace with my suffering.

I am in control of my need for alcohol.

I have the perfect amount of money available to me.

This last part of the exercise is a natural conclusion. You have started by recognising your fears. Your fears have helped you to identify more clearly what you really want. Now that you know what you want you can make a statement in the present moment that will help you to remember your truth. Your fears, which have helped you to get to this place, really can be said to have been a good thing!

Afterword

It has been nearly three years since I first started to write this book. It has been a powerful journey of self discovery for me and has enabled me to share and exchange ideas and stories with a fascinating mix of people.

I will probably want to go on rewriting this book for many years to come. Each time I have gone away from it and then read it again, often with the comments of other 'guinea-pigs' in mind, I have found myself almost disappointed at the limiting nature of words. There is so much to express, and yet so often when it comes to feeling, words seem to fall so short of the mark.

I wouldn't claim to have found all the answers. But I believe even more firmly as a result of this adventure and the men that I have come into contact with, that **you** can change your life if **you** want to.

Each time someone shares their story with me I become a witness to the enormous power we have to effect change if only we knew it. To share some of these stories, and some of the conclusions that I have come to as a result of my work, makes the writing of this book worthwhile.

I hope it enables you to see a little more clearly how your life reflects what has been, and is, going on inside you. If you've read **anything** which has helped to give you a clearer picture of your true identity, take this new knowledge with you into the world and see what you can do to start creating a life that more closely represents the man you really are.

About the Author

Barry Durdant-Hollamby lives with his wife, two children, father-in-law, and assorted pets in East Sussex, England. He spends his time being a father, husband, counsellor and writer (of books and music). Together with Shelley Sishton, he has

created The Art of Change, a body whose aims include helping individuals and groups to recognise and achieve their highest aspirations and purposes.

About The Art of Change

Change is a challenge in life. Nothing holds us back as much as our own limiting ideas and beliefs. Even the prospect of change can sometimes put us off attempting to do anything because the very idea seems so daunting.

The first, most important, step towards change in life is to know that you want to make it.

The Art of Change aims to guide people through the process, to manifest their highest potential and aspirations, helping to make it a smoother journey than maybe first imagined.

It does so with intuitive guidance from Barry Durdant-Hollamby, and the common sense application of tools such as meditation, visualisation, affirmations and the release of fears.

The Art of Change offers talks and workshops for groups of any size on subjects as far ranging as health issues, relationship problems, addictions, personal success, and financial abundance. The Art of Change can also consult with companies and organisations on similar themes.

More information about The Art of Change can be found at www.artofchange.co.uk.

E-mail us at: welcome@artofchange.co.uk

Other products available from The Art of Change:

Meditation and Visualisation audio tape

Containing an introduction to meditation and three visualisation techniques. Each exercise lasts approximately 20 minutes.

Stepping Stones

An easy-to-follow workbook offering practical guidance on managing the process of change in your life.

For full details of the above, or to join The Art of Change mailing information list, contact our web-site or write to:- The Art of Change, P.O. Box 441, EAST GRINSTEAD, RH18 5DH, stating your name, address and postcode.

Transparency

The Art of Change seeks to operate with complete transparency. That is, we aim to inform you of what our products have cost us to create and produce, and how much we may receive from the sale of our books and materials.

The Art of Change is being funded initially by benefactors who support our objectives and methods. The first publishing of this book has been funded entirely by such benefactors.

Costs incurred in the production and marketing of the initial publishing of The Male Agenda:-

Typesetting, artwork, supply and usage of the cover photograph, paper, printing, binding, support materials and media costs:
Approximately £3.50 per book

Retailer allowance:-
If you have bought this book from a shop, between 30% - 40% of the cover price is taken by the retailer:
Approximately £3.50 to the retailer per book

On this basis, selling at a price of £9.99 means The Art of Change receives around £3 per book sold.

Please note:-
The editing, proof-reading, cover design, layout ideas and typographical styles, marketing and promotional plans are being provided by experienced professionals who are giving their time free of charge.

Recommended Reading

Manhood and Raising Boys	*Steve Biddulph*
The Making of Love	*Steve & Shaaron Biddulph*
Unconditional Life	*Deepak Chopra*
Conversations With God Books 1, 2 & 3	*Neale Donald Walsch*
How to Meditate	*Eric Harrison*
Happiness Now! and Shift Happens!	*Robert Holden*
Under Saturn's Shadow	*James Hollis*
On Death And Dying	*Elisabeth Kübler-Ross*
Life After Life	*Raymond Moody*
Miracle On The 17th Green	*James Patterson & Peter de Jonge*
Do It!	*John-Roger & Peter McWilliams*
The Road Less Travelled	*M. Scott Peck*
The Game Of Life And How To Play It	*Florence Scovell-Shinn*
Do What You Love, The Money Will Follow	*Marsha Sinetar*